ARRAN

Robert McLellan
Revised by Norman Newton

David and Charles

ACKNOWLEDGEMENTS

Thanks to the Isle of Arran Tourist Board
for some of the photographs in this book.
The text of this book is, for the most
part, based on an excellent book written
by Robert McLellan for the David &
Charles 'Island' series, entitled The Island
of Arran, first published in 1970 and
updated by the author in 1976 and 1985.
Thanks to Mrs McLellan for permission
to use her late husband's text.

David & Charles is an imprint
of F&W Media International, Ltd
Brunel House, Forde Close,
Newton Abbot, TQ12 4PU, UK

F&W Media International, Ltd
is a subsidiary of F+W Media, Inc
10151 Carver Road, Suite #200,
Blue Ash, OH 45242, USA

First published in the UK in 1995
Reprinted 1996, 1999, 2001, 2003,
2004, 2008, 2012, 2015

A catalogue record for this book is
available from the British Library.

ISBN-13: 978-0-7153-2891-0 paperback
ISBN-10: 0-7153-2891-3 paperback

Printed in China
for David & Charles
Brunel House   Newton Abbot   Devon

F+W Media publishes high-quality
books on a wide range of subjects.
For more great book ideas visit:
www.fwmedia.com/uk

The Isle of
ARRAN

PEVENSEY
ISLAND GUIDES

ROBERT MCLELLAN

Revised by

NORMAN NEWTON

CONTENTS

Left: Auchagallon stone circle

Half title: Rubha Airigh Bheirg

Title page: Glen Catacol

1 SCOTLAND IN MINIATURE
A Circular Tour

I T IS 19 MILES (30km) from the Cock of Arran in the north of the island to Bennan Head in the south, 10 miles (16km) from Machrie Bay in the west to Corrygills Point in the east, and the island is estimated to cover an area of 165 square miles(427 square km). The population of Arran is around 4,700. The road round the island leaves the coast only in the north and south, and very briefly at the promontories of Clauchlands and Drumadoon; it is 56 miles (90km) long, and the coastline is estimated to be 60 miles long (96km). To drive round the whole island takes about two and a half hours. Two roads cross the island from east to west, high over the watershed, one from Brodick to Blackwaterfoot – the 'String Road' – and the other from Lamlash to Sliddery; yet the total length of the island roads is just short of 90 miles (145km).

All the fourteen settlements lie close to the coast, so the whole of the inhabited part of the island, and much of its unpopulated and wild interior, can be seen by a motorist in a single day. Even for the walker most of Arran is easily accessible, for although it will take many pleasant years to explore it thoroughly, it is quite possible to cross its wildest stretches in the course of a long summer day, and in a short day in winter you can reach a summit and still be back before dark.

Because of its small size, and the fact that it contains most of the features of the Highland and Lowland scenery of Scotland, Arran has been described by its local Tourist Board as 'Scotland in miniature' – though no part of it resembles the black midland belt which stretches on the mainland from the Clyde to the Forth, and contains nearly all the industry, and most of the population, of mainland Scotland. Nor has any part of the island anything in common with the fertile low farmlands of the Lothians or the eastern coastal counties between the Forth and the Moray Firth. Nowadays regarded as one of the Clyde islands, Arran is, nevertheless, Hebridean in character, particularly on the west side, and indeed geologically, historically and culturally it has affinities with the Inner Hebrides, and even with Ireland.

The three main villages on the east coast, Brodick, Lamlash and Whiting Bay, are fairly typical small coastal resorts, with almost a suburban character of comparatively recent development. But the rest of Arran is of

TURF DYKES TO TRIDENT

Everywhere in the upper glens are the ruins of old black-houses and turf dykes. In the straths or on the shores are the little oblong sites of ancient chapels. On the hilltops around the coast are faint traces of fortifications, and on the moors are standing stones, stone circles and chambered cairns. All this on the same island as stone-built Victorian hotels and villas, brick and rough-cast boarding houses built in the 1930s, and more recent bungalows of pre-cast concrete and coloured tiles, all of which dominate the main villages. In the same world, too, as the nuclear power station across the Firth of Clyde at Hunterston, the oil tanks at Ardrossan, the Trident submarines coming and going from their base further up the Clyde at Coulport, and the contrails of jet planes overhead on the flight path to North America. The contrasts create a perspective in which past and present alike take their place, under the eye of eternity.

Left: Glen Shurig and Goatfell from the String Road

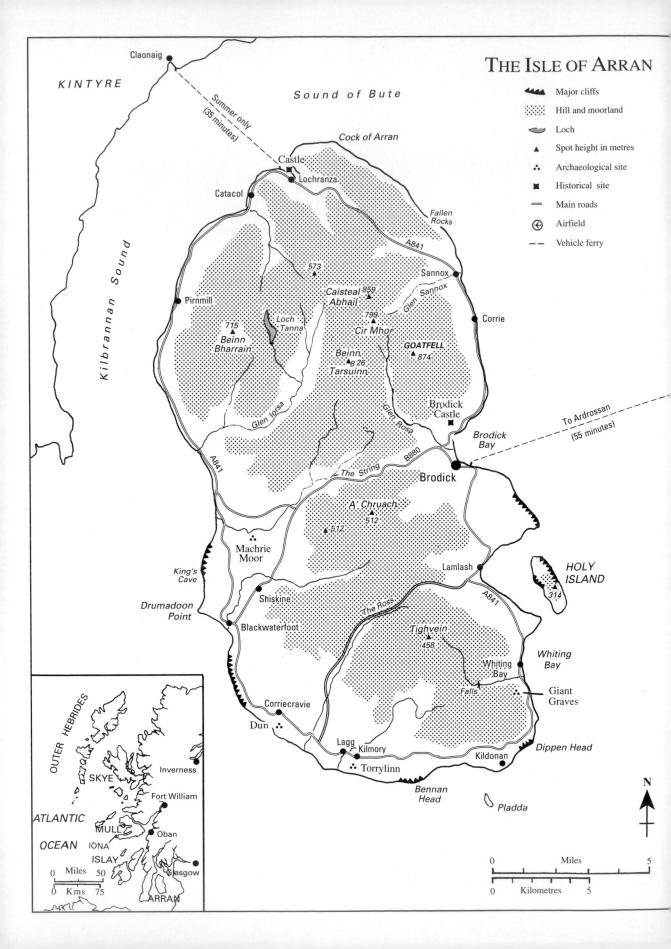

THE ISLE OF ARRAN

Legend:
- Major cliffs
- Hill and moorland
- Loch
- ▲ Spot height in metres
- ∴ Archaeological site
- ◼ Historical site
- Main roads
- ⊕ Airfield
- Vehicle ferry

KINTYRE

Sound of Bute

Claonaig

Summer only
(35 minutes)

Cock of Arran

Castle
Lochranza

Catacol

Fallen Rocks

A841

573

Sannox

Caisteal 859
Abhail

Glen Sannox

Corrie

Pirnmill

Kilbrannan Sound

715
Beinn
Bharrain

Loch
Tanna

799

Cir Mhor

Beinn
Tarsuinn 826

GOATFELL
874

Glen Iorsa

Glen Rosa

Brodick
Castle

To Ardrossan
(55 minutes)

Brodick
Bay

A841

The String

B880

Brodick

A' Chruach
512

512

Machrie
Moor

HOLY
ISLAND

King's
Cave

Lamlash

314

Drumadoon
Point

Shiskine

The Ross

A841

Blackwaterfoot

Tighvein
458

Whiting
Bay

Whiting
Bay

Giant
Graves

Falls

Corriecravie

Dippen Head

Dun

Lagg
Kilmory

Torrylinn

Kildonan

Bennan
Head

Pladda

N

OUTER HEBRIDES

SKYE

Inverness

ATLANTIC

Fort William

OCEAN

MULL

Oban

IONA

ISLAY

Glasgow

ARRAN

0   Miles   50

0   Kms   75

0   Miles   5

0   Kilometres   5

Storm over Kintyre from Brown Head

a pattern established after the Clearances of the early nineteenth century, one which is common to all the Highlands and Islands, and to Ireland. It is a Celtic landscape, although this would more accurately describe the landscape pattern which the Clearances destroyed. White farmhouses lie irregularly by the little fields of the coastal strip and the lower inland waters, with open hillside behind, and mountain peaks in the distance. There is indeed a Celtic quality in the whole island environment, in spite of changes in social organisation and language, and the arrival of new settlers in recent times. It carries, like Yeats's Ireland, a sense of the present co-existing with a past so remote as to stretch beyond history into legend. Almost every feature of the landscape has a name in Gaelic or Norse. The Gaelic language is sadly almost forgotten on Arran, although its accent lingers.

Clearances Monument, Lamlash

Many visitors coming to Arran for the first time will be familiar with its jagged silhouette, and many maintain that the best view of Arran is the distant one. Robert Burns is said to have been blind to natural grandeur because he could see Arran almost daily from the Ayrshire farms on which he spent his youth, although he never once mentioned it either in verse or prose. Perhaps, viewing the distant hills from inland Ayrshire, he was unaware that he was viewing a separate island, but from anywhere on the coastline of the Firth of Clyde it makes an immediate impact. Lying 15 miles (24km) or so across the water, Arran is lofty and jagged in the north, undulating in the middle, and sloping in the south, its sides gashed by narrow glens, its coastline broken by the steep shape of Holy Isle, and given added variety at its southern extreme by the outline of the low islet of Pladda; it dominates every other natural feature in view, drawing the eye from the waters of the firth to its summit peaks, then up to the blue of the sky, or into

GETTING THERE

There are two ways of approaching Arran. The main car ferry, operated by Caledonian MacBrayne, sails from Ardrossan in Ayrshire to Brodick, Arran's main town, situated halfway down the east side of the island; in good weather the crossing takes fifty-five minutes. During winter storms the ferry sometimes diverts to the more sheltered pier at Gourock.

Alternatively, a small seasonal car ferry crosses from Claonaig on the north-east coast of Kintyre, beyond Skipness, to the village of Lochranza on the north-west tip of Arran. This crossing takes about thirty minutes. For the Ardrossan ferry, booking is advisable; for the Kintyre ferry, be prepared to wait in a queue during busy periods.

The ferry at Brodick

the clouds. Spiritually, as well as in a literal sense, the sight is uplifting.

From the east coast of the Kintyre peninsula, Glaswegians are surprised to see a mirror image of the profile they are used to. And from a much closer vantage point, only 4 miles away (6.5km) across Kilbrannan Sound, every detail of the fields and whitewashed cottages on the Arran shore can be seen, and the high peaks behind. From the fort of Dunagoil in the south-west of the island of Bute, at sunset on a winter's evening, the northern peaks of Arran seem to be heightened and intensified by the luminosity of the hidden sun, providing an inspirational experience. Indeed it has been said that Bute is superior to Arran in only one respect, that the view of Arran from Bute surpasses that of Bute from Arran.

A CIRCULAR TOUR

AFTER ARRIVING IN ARRAN and settling into your accommodation, you may wish to undertake an exploratory tour of the island. Starting from Brodick and proceeding in a clockwise direction, you cross moorland inland from Corrygills Point and then the first village encountered is Lamlash, sheltering behind the bulk of Holy Island. Both Lamlash and the next village to the south, Whiting Bay, are tourist resorts, with many guesthouses, bed-and-breakfast accommodation, tourist services, craft shops, tearooms, and all the paraphernalia of the tourist industry. But beyond Whiting Bay you enter into a Hebridean world of small crofting townships, whitewashed cottages, beautiful coastline, peace, tranquillity and empty space.

On the southern coast of Arran are the tiny villages of Dippen and Kildonan, from where there is a fine view south down the Firth of Clyde over the tiny island of Pladda with its lighthouse to Ailsa Craig and the Ayrshire coast. Continuing past Bennan Head, the most southerly point of Arran, you come to the villages of Kilmory and Lagg. The palm trees at Lagg Inn, and the sheltered tea garden, make this a popular stopping place on the Arran circuit.

Just before Sliddery, the next village, you pass the road which runs through Glen Scorrodale and over the hill to Lamlash. Continue round the coast road, through Corriecravie and Kilpatrick and then you will reach the most substantial settlement on the west side of Arran, Blackwaterfoot. This is a wonderfully picturesque little village, with an attractive harbour, stone bridge, hotels and shops. Drumadoon Point, to the west of Blackwaterfoot, is a popular area for moderately adventurous visitors, with dramatic geology, interesting wildlife, prehistoric hill fort and the 'King's Cave' as attractions. To the west is Kintyre, a low-lying and monotonous peninsula as seen from Arran, its profile broken only by the irregularities of Saddell Bay and Campbeltown Loch, guarded by Davaar Island. To the south of Kintyre is the little island of Sanda.

Through Shiskine and keeping to the coast, the road comes to Torbeg and then Tormore, crosses the Machrie water and reaches the village of Machrie. In recent years the prehistoric attractions of this part of Arran have been more thoroughly investigated, and so have become more widely known. On Machrie Moor there are standing stones, stone circles and hut circles dating from the Bronze Age. Four thousand years ago this was one of the most important ritual landscapes in Bronze Age Britain, matching the Kilmartin valley in Argyll to the north, and even the plains around Stonehenge in Wessex.

Machrie lies halfway up the west side of Arran and is connected to Brodick by the 'String Road' across the middle of the island, planned by Thomas Telford and built in 1817 although today's version is, of course, wider and faster than the original. On the west coast north of Machrie lies the least populated part of the island, the road passing through the former herring fishing village of Pirnmill, through Catacol to Lochranza with its ancient, photogenic castle and modern ferry pier.

One of the many stone circles on Machrie Moor, an important ritual centre during the prehistoric Bronze Age (Isle of Arran Tourist Board)

Here our route cuts inland again, running up Glen Chalmadale and rejoining the east coast at Sannox. The more intrepid can walk to the north headland of the island, the Cock of Arran, from where they can look over to the island of Bute and the hills of Cowal and mid-Argyll. Heading south the road comes to Corrie, considered by Mr Asquith to be one of the prettiest villages in Europe. Most of its houses are now holiday cottages.

The road runs along the coast past Brodick Castle and gardens, past the eastern end of the String Road, past the excellent Arran Heritage Museum, and finally arriving at the town of Brodick.

After this whirlwind tour of Arran let us now take the opportunity to explore its constituent parts in more depth, starting with its capital, Brodick, with diversions along the way into something of the history, geology, archaeology, and ecology of this fascinating place. Part of the appeal of any island is being able to leave the mainland behind, with all the hustle and bustle which that entails for most of us. Coming to an island, especially by ferry, puts us in an ideal position to appreciate the natural environment, and one of Arran's most appealing features is the extraordinary variety of its very attractive landscape.

Overleaf: Mountain range from the A841, half-a-mile south of Brodick with Goatfell on the right

GEOLOGY

HUTTON'S HOT ROCK

The island has an important place in the history of the science of geology for it was to Arran's dramatic scenery that James Hutton, the father of igneous geology, came at the end of the eighteenth century for evidence in favour of his view that some rocks are not a result of the hardening and subsequent transformation of sediments accumulated at the bottom of the sea, but were formed by the cooling and hardening of molten material forced up from within the earth by eruptions of immense power. During his lifetime Hutton's views were treated with scorn and sarcasm by his academic colleagues, but we now know that his insights were correct.

EVEN IF you are not an enthusiastic amateur geologist, it is worth making the effort to understand how Arran's scenery came to be the way it is; the Arran Heritage Museum has an excellent display on the subject.

Arran's present appearance is the result of millions of years of geological activity. The eroding influences of frost and wind and running water are obvious in the denuded sides of the peaks, the masses of tumbled rock in the corrie bottoms, the exposed outcrops in the glens, and the level deposits of mud or sand or gravel through which the larger waters wind to the sea. Even to the uninitiated, the U-shaped glens of the northern rivers and streams, the hanging tributary corries, the scored rock surfaces, and the presence almost everywhere of precariously balanced gigantic boulders, in shapes and positions inexplicable in terms of common weather erosion or of the force of gravity, combine to suggest the agency of some powerful force no longer active, perhaps ancient ice. Moreover the strip of level land around the coast, on which the motorist often travels, arouses at least a suspicion that in a more recent past the sea was at a higher level than it is today.

The striking northern granite peaks of Arran are the eroded remnants of a great mass of molten material which welled up from the fiery interior of the earth, pushing up the existing layers of rock to form a gigantic blister. Protected by these upper layers from the chill of the atmosphere, the mass cooled so slowly as to produce the large crystals characteristic of granite. Eventually, cooled and hardened, the great dome-shaped mass was exposed to the air once the layers of older and softer rock above it were eroded away.

The tremendous extent of this erosion is made plain when we consider another characteristic feature of the island landscape, the basaltic dykes which exist in such large numbers, particularly in the south where they are everywhere exposed along the coast. These vertical walls of dark rock, running from the inland cliffs along the foreshore and out across the sand into the sea, are the result of molten material forcing its way up through cracks in the earth's crust. In this case the molten rock cooled quickly, producing the distinctive basalt formations which now dominate a shore composed of sand derived from the softer surrounding rocks by the action of the sea.

Thus if the great eroded granite dome is the dominant feature of the north end of Arran, it is the basaltic dykes which are most prominent in the south. From Drumadoon Point in the west to Clauchlands Point in the east, and especially at the cliffs of Brown Head, Bennan Head and Dippen Head, and on Holy Isle, the most impressive natural features of the southern landscape are the igneous rocks intruded in a molten state between the layers of softer sedimentary rocks already in existence.

The latest dykes were formed in a period of igneous activity sixty-five million years ago, which in geological terms is regarded as recent. The oldest rocks in Arran, the schists, have existed for over five hundred million years.

However, even more recent geological processes have left their mark, as a series of ice ages or glaciations has sculpted the island into the familiar profiles we admire today.

Arran had its own ice sheet, strong enough to fend off the ice rivers which gouged out Kilbrannan Sound and the Firth of Clyde. In the process it moulded and sculpted the peaks and glens into roughly their present shape, the proof of this being found over the whole southern half of the island where huge blocks of the northern granite can be found, and also on the eastern and western coastal fringes where granite blocks have been deposited by the ice, moved miles from their original locations.

Apart from these stray boulders, or glacial erratics, and the typically glaciated valley shapes, the main evidence of the ice ages lies in the presence of raised beaches visible around the island. There are three main levels, at 100 feet (30m), 50 feet (15m) and 25 feet (7.5m), formed at the close of the Ice Age when melting ice led to a rise in sea level and thus the forming of beaches. The land had been pushed down by the weight of thousands of feet of ice, and when the ice melted, the land began to rise up slowly, through a process known as isostatic recovery.

Arran is therefore classic ground for the geologist, and because of this and because it contains within practicable bounds a fairly complete synopsis of the geology of Scotland – a 'Scotland in miniature' – demonstrating the contrast between the Highland formations in the north and those of the Lowland in the south, it is now visited every year, especially at Easter, by hundreds of students and their teachers, who erupt from the boarding houses and hostels equipped with knapsack and hammer to assist nature in the work of erosion. The evidence of their hammering is most obvious where interest is concentrated into a relatively small area, as in North Glen Sannox, where rocks between the schists and old red sandstones are exposed in the burn below the North Sannox bridge. Along the Corrie shore and along the north coast of Arran between Corloch and the Cock of Arran the carboniferous series is well displayed, and at certain times students swarm over this area.

In the Corrygills area pitchstone occurs, a glassy volcanic rock used in prehistoric times as an alternative to flint, and specimens can be collected at the point where an igneous sill is exposed, about 90 yards (100m) downstream from the point at which the South Corrygills road crosses the southern branch of the Corrygills burn, and also from the point where the same sill crosses the shore to the south-east.

Iorsa Water

Overleaf: The String – from the top of the pass looking west

15

2 THE HAMILTON DUKES AND GOATFELL
A Guide to Brodick Bay

TWO EDIFICES DOMINATE the wide expanse of Brodick Bay: one is the impressive castle, dating from the thirteenth century and built by feudal lords, and the other is Goatfell, the massive peak overlooking Brodick Bay, millions of years old and erected by the forces of nature. In their different ways they are equally impressive.

The mountain's name is Norse, Geita-fjall or 'goat mountain', at a height of 2,866 feet (873.5m) the highest peak on the island. The history of the castle encompasses not only the human history of Arran over recent centuries, but also that of the kingdom of Scotland, in which its owners played important parts at different times.

It is known that sometime in the thirteenth century, before the battle of Largs in 1263, Angus MacDonald, Lord of the Isles, and his uncle Ruari MacRanald, ancestor of the MacGrories of Bute, had garrisoned the castles of Rothesay, Lamlash and Brodick against Alexander the High Steward, who claimed Bute and Arran through his marriage with a granddaughter of Angus, son of Somerled. After the cession of the Western Isles of Scotland to Alexander III, Bute and Arran were brought formally into the kingdom of Scotland, by which time the Stewart claim to the island had the authority of a feudal right.

The feudal system was introduced into Scotland in the reign of David I, after which the king instituted the practice of making grants of land to his earls, who in turn could grant land to barons, who could grant it to knights, all of whom had to have their grants approved by the king, and all of whom were vassals of the king as well as of their immediate feudal superiors. This was a big change from the traditional Celtic system, under which the king was elected by the chiefs and the chiefs by their own kindred, who also owned the land. So it was that the Scottish king was not the ultimate owner of the land but the leader of his people, and was known as a king of Scots, rather than a king of Scotland.

Brodick Castle gardens

ARRAN IN BARBOUR'S *THE BRUCE*

BRODICK CASTLE first surfaces in written sources early in the fourteenth century during the Scottish War of Independence, the struggle by Robert the Bruce against the English which culminated in victory at the battle of Bannockburn in 1314. In the early years of the war, when Bruce's support on the mainland was precarious, he took refuge on the island of Rathlin, off the northern coast of Ireland in the winter of 1306–7. The story of Bruce's struggle was told in verse by John Barbour, Archdeacon of Aberdeen, in a chronicle entitled *The Bruce*. Barbour lived from 1316 to 1395 and so was not an eyewitness of the events he describes, but he was writing at a time when people who had participated in the events were still alive, and he had met and talked to some of them. His aim was to tell the truth as far as he knew it, and although his work has a natural bias in favour of his hero, it is not a romance

Left: Brodick Bay with the peak of Goatfell on the right

like Scott's *Lord of the Isles*, a poem written in 1814 and covering the same events, in which poetic licence is taken without scruple. It is a reasonably sober verse chronicle, conflicting in no important essential with any other available evidence.

This aspect is stressed because the chronicle provides the only nearly contemporary account of Bruce's adventures in Arran, and in view of the extent to which these have been embroidered by tradition, it is interesting to note exactly what it says. After Bruce had wintered in Rathlin – where it is understood he found encouragement in the attempts of a spider to spin its web – he was approached by Sir James Douglas and Sir Robert Boyd for permission to take a party and visit Arran, in the hope that they might be able to strike a blow against the English governor of Brodick Castle.

Douglas and Boyd left Rathlin with a small party of men in a single galley but without Bruce, crossed to Kintyre and 'rowit all-wayis by the land' until night was near, when they crossed over to Arran.

> And under ane bra thair galay dreuch,
> And syne it helit weill ineuch;
> Thair takill, ayris, and thair stere,
> Thai hyde all on the samyn maner.
> And held thair way rycht in the nycht,
> Sa that, or day wes dawn lycht,
> Thai war enbuschit the castell neir,
> Arrayit on the best maneir.

It would seem from this – it helps to recount it out loud – that they landed somewhere in the west of the island and drew their galley up under a brae, or hillside. They 'helit' (covered) it, and hid their tackle, oars, and rudder in the same way, and then immediately made their way across the island by night, to arrive in the vicinity of Brodick Castle just before dawn.

It happened by chance that the under-warden of the castle had the previous evening brought to the shore below it three boats containing provisions, clothing and arms, and which a party of over thirty men were just beginning to unload. Douglas and his men attacked and overcame them. The sound of the fighting was heard in the castle and more men were sent to attempt a rescue, but Douglas saw them coming and went to meet them.

> And quhen thai of the castell saw
> Hym cum on thaim forouten aw,
> Thai fled forouten mair debate;
> Amd thai thame followed to the yhate,
> And slew of thame, as thai in past;
> Bot thai thair yhet barrit so fast,
> At thai mycht do at thame no mair;
> Tarfor thai left thame ilkane thair,
> And turnit to the see againe.

In other words, Douglas chased the castle party back to the gate, which was shut against them so 'fast' (tightly) that he could do no more, so he turned to the sea again.

Back on the shore Douglas found that the three unloaded boats had put to sea, but the wind was so strong that the crews could hardly row against it, and two were wrecked. The arms, clothing and provisions – 'wyne and othir thing' – which had been unloaded were seized by Douglas and his men, who 'held thair way, rycht glad and joyful of thair pray'. Where they went we cannot be quite certain, but it was 'till a strenth', that is, to some sort of stronghold; a later reference describes it as having been in a 'woddy glen'. The only 'strength' both near Brodick Castle and in a woody glen would be the old fort near the head of Glencloy, and it would, of course, have been in ruins even then, since it dated from either the prehistoric period or was just possibly a structure rebuilt after the Viking occupation by the Lords of the Isles; but there must have been enough of it left to have afforded some protection, and in any case the site would have been a defence in itself.

Ten days later, to continue the story told by Barbour's chronicle, Bruce himself arrived in Arran with thirty small galleys. Where he landed we can only guess. The chronicle says:

> The King arrivit in Arane;
> And syne to the land is gane,
> And in a toune tuk his herbery.

By 'toune' is meant a *baile*, a *clachan* or small village composed of the dwellings and outbuildings of a *runrig* farm community. Which 'toune' in Arran is indicated again we can only guess, but since there is no mention later in the chronicle of Bruce having moved his fleet before he left the island, it seems likely that he landed on the east coast, possibly at Whiting Bay, or in the bay opposite Holy Isle, at what is now Lamlash. Exchequer rolls of 1449, some 140 years later, list farm communities in the area at 'Knokanelze, Achinarn, Ardlavenys, Monymor, Penycroce, Latternaguanach, Blarebeg, Blaremore, Dowbrowach, Marcynegles and Clachan', represented today in all but two cases by the names Knockankelly, Auchencairn, Monamore, King's Cross, Letter, Blairbeg, Blairmore, Margnaheglish and Clauchlands. The change of the name Penycroce to King's Cross is the result of a tradition linking that place with Bruce's visit, and if he did take shelter in the 'toune' at King's Cross it is likely that his fleet was drawn up on the shore at Whiting Bay during the period of his stay on the island.

When Bruce had taken up his quarters in the 'toune' he

> ...small sperit syne full specialy,
> Giff ony man couth tell tithand,
> Of any strangers in that land.

A woman told him that their governor had recently been discomfited by a party of strangers who were at the time encamped in a 'stalward place

heirby'. He told her that the men were his and asked her to show him the place. This is curious, for even if his fleet had been in Lamlash Bay, the walk to the old fort in Glencloy would have been long enough to justify his asking for a man to guide him. Later in the story we learn that his 'hostes', who may or may not have been the same woman, had two sons who joined Bruce's company. The fact that a man was not asked to guide Bruce to the camp of Douglas may suggest that on the arrival of Bruce's fleet the men of the island had taken to the hills until they learned that it was safe to return. On being shown the 'sted' in the 'woddy glen' where Douglas had camped, Bruce blew his horn three times in a way recognised by Douglas and Boyd, who joined him, and returned with him to his 'herbery', or quarters in the 'toune'.

In Barbour's version, Bruce then decides to send Cuthbert, a native of Carrick, across the Firth of Clyde to find out if it was held by friends or enemies, and to light a fire on Turnberry Point if it was safe to proceed with the fleet and make a landing. How it came about that on the prearranged day a farmer was burning straw, and what then happened, is not relevant to what happened on Arran, but the story does tend to confirm that Bruce's fleet was in Whiting Bay, as Turnberry is visible from there but not from Lamlash.

Clearly Brodick Castle was not captured by Bruce, as this is not mentioned by Barbour. Nor is there any mention of any stay by Bruce in the 'King's Cave' at Drumadoon, nor is such a stay likely, since it is explicitly stated that he had quarters in the 'toune' near which he landed. Some men of Douglas's advance party, however, must surely have gone back to the west coast to retrieve the galley they had hidden there, and these may have spent some days in the cave at Drumadoon. The association of the cave with Bruce may therefore have some justification.

The woman who sent her two sons to Carrick with Bruce is described as his 'hostes'. She claimed to have second sight, and told him that he would ultimately succeed and free his kingdom, sending her sons with him to show her faith in her own powers of prophecy, and hinting that she expected them to be well rewarded. Bruce was somewhat comforted by what she said:

> The-quhethir he trowit nocht full weill
> Hir spek, for he had gret ferly
> How scho suld wit it sekirly.

In other words, he did not altogether believe her, for he wondered how she could be so certain. The sending of the two sons and the hint at the reward expected is all that is to be found in Barbour in support of the local tradition that several of the oldest Arran families, in particular the Fullartons of Kilmichael in Glencloy, were granted lands in Arran by Bruce in recognition of the loyal service they gave him during this particular visit to the island. This is not recorded by Martin Martin in 1695, but it is repeated regularly since the visit of Pennant in 1772. Who his 'hostes' was we do not know, nor if her two sons lived to be rewarded. Unfortunately there is no record of any grant by Bruce of land on the island to any Arran man.

GOATFELL

If Brodick Castle is Arran's most important building, easily the most important natural feature on the island is Goatfell, the highest mountain and also the most prominent. It is only 2,866 feet (873.5m), but on a clear day walkers will be rewarded by a wonderful, panoramic view over Argyll and Ayrshire and the surrounding islands. Well-marked paths to the summit of Goatfell start from Claddach, High Corrie and Brodick Castle – though beware, as the weather can change quickly and visitors should not attempt the ascent, straightforward though it is, without proper footwear, adequate warm clothing and raingear, and spare food. If conditions do deteriorate, don't be afraid to turn back; and before you even start always let somebody know where you are going and when you expect to be back.

Left: The broad sweep of Brodick Bay, looking north over the town to Goatfell (Isle of Arran Tourist Board)

Previous page: King's Caves

Overleaf: Rubha Airigh Bheirg – two miles south-west of Catacol

STEWARTS AND HAMILTONS

NORMANS AND MACDONALDS

Various parts of the island were granted to Norman families, but it is interesting to see the Lord of the Isles – effectively an independent baron whose lineage caused untold trouble for successive Scottish kings – making a grant of land at Shiskine to the monastery at Saddell just across the water on the east coast of Kintyre. Saddell Abbey was started during the time of Somerled, and completed by his son Reginald, or Ranald, whose son Donald became the leader of Clan Donald, from whom the millions of MacDonalds in the world take their name.

AFTER THE MATTER of the independence of Scotland was settled at Bannockburn in 1314, Arran became once again the property of the Stewarts. When the younger branch of the Stewart family failed to produce a male heir, Robert the High Steward – son of Walter who was the young warrior of Bannockburn and the husband of Bruce's daughter Marjory – took the lands of Knapdale and Arran back into his own possession. Later this Robert was to become Robert II of Scotland, as the grandson of Bruce.

During the later Middle Ages Arran proved difficult to rule. Administratively it was part of the sheriffdom of Bute, and was a bailiery, ruled by a bailie who was the sheriff's deputy. He may have occupied Brodick Castle, and he seems usually to have been a Stewart, like the sheriff. In 1609 responsibility for keeping the peace on Arran, and for the administration of justice, was conferred on the first Marquis of Hamilton beginning an association with the island which lasted until recent times. The history of Arran became closely linked with the fortunes of the Stewart dynasty, and their Hamilton supporters.

In 1351 Brodick Castle was destroyed by an English raiding party, and again in 1406. In the fifteenth century supporters of the Lords of the Isles on several occasions attacked farms held by charters from the Scottish Crown,

and again destroyed the castle at Brodick (presumably repaired and rebuilt) in 1455.

So, Brodick Castle has a long and complicated history, which to some extent can be unravelled by a visit there. It is well looked after by the National Trust for Scotland, who also keep the extensive gardens in good order. The Victorian wing of the castle was added in 1844, completing a process started two hundred years before when a Cromwellian garrison was in control of what was one of the last royal castles in Scotland to hold out. In 1649 both Charles I and the first Duke of Hamilton were executed, but the Hamilton family regained the estates at the Restoration.

The Hamilton lands in Arran passed on the death of the 12th Duke of Hamilton to his only child, the Lady Mary Louise, who in 1906 married the Marquis of Graham, later to become the 6th Duke of Montrose. On her death in 1957, which followed only three years after that of her husband, Brodick Castle and gardens became the property of the Treasury in part payment of death duties, and the Treasury presented them to the National Trust for Scotland. Most of the other lands in Arran belonging to the Hamiltons have been disposed of, either gifted or sold; for example, 7,000 acres (2,833 hectares) in the Goatfell and Glen Rosa area were presented to the National Trust for Scotland.

It is well worthwhile visiting Brodick Castle, especially if one's appreciation of the history of the island is seen not only here in the changing fortunes of its most powerful families, but also by a visit to the Arran Heritage Museum, on the edge of Brodick, where the history of the ordinary people of Arran is displayed.

BRODICK

THE TOWN OF BRODICK has all the facilities any visitor could possibly need. It is the largest settlement and the main port of entry, and has mushroomed in recent years. The population of Arran is around 4,000, with an increasing concentration in Brodick, to the detriment of other parts of the island. However, it is worth remembering that in the 1960s the declining population seemed to call into question the island's very survival as a viable community; happily the gloomy predictions of that time have been avoided, in part due to an influx of people settling on the island, also to the growth of tourism which has become its most important industry, along with the encouragement of a variety of small-scale enterprises, all of which provide much-needed employment in a fragile community.

Left: Isle of Arran Heritage Mueum, Brodick

Cup-and-ring marked rock above Brodick

Detail of the grave of John Adams-Acton and his wife, Jeanie Hering, Brodick

3 Vikings, Saints, Buddhists and Mustard
Lamlash and Holy Isle

DRIVING SOUTH OUT OF BRODICK, the road climbs up on to moorland, giving fine views of the town and Brodick Bay. Soon the small coastal resort of Lamlash comes into view, at the head of a large bay sheltered by the steep bulk of Holy Isle. Lamlash is a centre for water sports of all kinds, and has the usual craft shops and tearooms to cater for its tourist traffic. The golf course has magnificent views across to Holy Isle. The island's hospital, the Arran War Memorial Hospital, the High School, and local government offices are also located in Lamlash.

LAMLASH

THE NAME OF THE VILLAGE is the clue to the history of this part of Arran. One of the kings of Dalriada had a daughter who married an Irish chieftain, and gave birth to a son, Las, who became one of the many Irish monks who brought Christianity to the west coast of Scotland in the sixth century AD. Las was born in 566, and died in 639, by that time the Abbot of Leithglinn in Leinster. As a young monk, just after completing his formal education in Ireland, he came to a cave on what is now Holy Island to spend, like the young Christ and in the fashion of his time, a period in the wilderness.

Las had the common prefix *mo*, meaning 'my', attached to his name, as was often the case with holy men, and became known as Molas. Dean Monro, writing after a visit to Arran in 1549, referred to Holy Isle as the 'yle of Molass'. Its Gaelic name was Eilean Molaise, from *eilean*, 'island', and *Molaise*, 'of Molas', and this has been corrupted through Elmolaise and Lemolash to Lamlash, which was the name of Holy Isle before 1830, after which it became attached to the village then developing on the shore of the bay opposite.

It is very unlikely that St Molaise, or Molas, introduced Christianity into Arran. St Ninian, who certainly visited Sanda to the south and Bute to the north, died around AD424, and St Brendan, after whom Kilbrannan Sound is named, was active in the area some thirty or forty years before Molaise.

St Molas stone in wall of Shiskine Church

Top left: Holy Island with Lamlash golf course in the foreground

Bottom left: Lamlash

DALRIADA AND THE SCOTS

IT IS SIGNIFICANT that in Lamlash, a name commemorating the visit of a monk, Arran has its single link with a member of the kindred of Gabran, its Dalriadic owners. Sometime towards the end of the fifth century AD a group of people called Scotti by the Romans came over from the small kingdom of Dalriada in Northern Ireland to found a kingdom in the south-west of Scotland, in what became known as Argyll. In most places they displaced Picts as the ruling élite, though probably the native population remained. They brought with them a new language, Gaelic, which they

Hamilton Terrace, Lamlash

introduced into what would later become Scotland. Most Arran place-names are Gaelic, with some Norse additions.

The territory of the kingdom of Dalriada corresponded roughly to the present Argyll, stretching from the Mull of Kintyre to the south-western end of the Great Glen, and from Drumalban westward to Islay and Jura. With the arrival of these first 'Scots' we are on the threshold of history, having various king lists, annals and chronicles to add to the evidence of archaeology and place-names, although for the first centuries of the occupation evidence is still slight, and much of it recorded some time after events, and later copied and re-copied, so the early historical evidence has to be approached cautiously.

The story is told that the Scottish kingdom of Dalriada was founded by the three sons of Erc, King of Dalriada in Northern Ireland. The three brothers were Angus, Lorn and Fergus. From Fergus was descended Kenneth MacAlpin who in 844 became the first king of the united kingdom of the Picts and the Scots. The kindred of Angus occupied Islay and Jura, the kindred of Lorn settled in the northern part of Argyll in the district that now bears his name, while the kindred of Gabran, a grandson of Fergus, took Knapdale, Kintyre, Bute and Arran.

War graves in Kilbride cemetery above Lamlash

VIKINGS

THIS WAS THE SITUATION in south-west Scotland when the Vikings arrived. The first recorded Viking raid in the west of Scotland was at Iona, in AD795, and many others followed over the next fifty years. These early raids were not attempts at colonisation, or conquest: they were crude acts of piracy. The raiders were followers of Odin, not Christianity, and the monasteries attracted them because of their treasures. Lindisfarne, a daughter monastery of Iona, was raided as early as AD793, and Iona in 802 and 806. After further raids Iona was abandoned, and the monks retreated to Ireland, taking their treasures with them, including most probably what is now known as the *Book of Kells*. But Ireland received the attention of the Vikings too, and many of its monasteries were ravaged, by men who would tear the gold mountings from a beautifully illuminated manuscript gospel and throw the book away. Yet even the most ruthless of them were subdued in the end, not by the sword, but by the cross, and some of them died as monks.

That Arran suffered in the early raids is almost certain. The evidence of the Viking impact on the island comes partly from archaeology, partly from place-names, and partly from chronicles and sagas. A grave mound at Lamlash, now destroyed, produced a shield boss of exactly the type found in Norway in grave mounds of the late eighth or the early ninth century, so it was considered to have covered one of the earliest Viking burials in Scotland. If the dating is sound, it seems probable that the Viking who met his end at Lamlash was from the fleet which raided Kintyre in AD797, and if there was a monastery at Kilpatrick, as that place-name suggests, it may well have been that fleet which closed its history.

Another Viking burial lies under a boat-shaped mound, to the landward side of the small round fort on King's Cross Point. In it were found the rivets of a ship and a coin which was minted between AD837 and 854.

Magnus Barelegs certainly claimed Arran at the end of the eleventh century, when he concluded an agreement with the Scottish king, allowing the Norwegians sovereignty over all the west coast islands which they could sail around. It seems most probable that Arran was occupied throughout the Viking period. From the evidence of place-names it appears that the earlier population was not to any extent supplanted and replaced by Norse settlers, as happened in the Outer Hebrides and in Islay.

The Vikings gave their own names to the more prominent features of the landscape, as with Geita-fjall, 'goat mountain'; and some of the main bays, as Sandvik, 'sand bay', in Gaelic Sannaig, now Sannox, and Breidavik, 'broad bay', now Brodick. There are no farm or village names in Norse, but many of the glens have obviously been long enough settled by Vikings to retain the memory in their 'dale' endings, and several such as Glen Chalmadale, Glen Scorradale and Ormidale may even commemorate the name of the settler. But the most certain indication of the nature of the Norse occupation comes from a group of place-names which are not Norse but Gaelic.

These are the farm or field names which indicate that a Gaelic-speaking population paid rent to Viking overlords. In Dalriadic times the unit on which dues were paid to the chief was a standard *baile* or village of twenty houses, each house having land for twenty-one cows and their followers, and paying the value equivalent of three cows in rent. Traces of this system, which was introduced from Ireland, survive throughout Dalriada in the place-names, and it was almost certainly used in Arran, too.

NORSE OR GAELIC

Some prominent Arran place-names the Vikings adapted to their own Norse, as with the Gaelic Eilean Molaise which became Mallasey of Melansay, the suffix 'ey' being Norse for 'island'. The name Arran itself, in modern Gaelic Arainn, they called Herrey or Hersey, and this too has been interpreted as an adaptation, meaning either 'lofty island' or 'stag island', according to which Gaelic original they are attributed. The manipulation of place-names is a pleasant pursuit, but until some meaning can be suggested which fits Arran equally with the island of Aran off the coast of Donegal, and the Aran Islands off Galway, it would be wise to regard the derivation as unsolved. The Irish islands are neither noticeably lofty nor populated by red deer, and are not likely ever to have been so.

Cross and font, Lamlash church

In Arran, where the more fertile land is scattered in limited pockets, larger communities would be comparatively rare, and we should expect to find place-names prefixed with 'kerry' or 'auchter', from *cearadh* meaning 'quarter' and *ochda* meaning 'eighth', denoting a quarter or an eighth of a standard *baile*. We can deduce little from the fact that there are several place-names prefixed by 'bal' or 'bally', as at Balnacoole, Ballygowan, Ballymeanoch and Ballygonachie, for the word *baile* came to denote simply a village, standard or not. What is more significant is that there are no place-names in Arran with the prefix 'kerry' or 'auchter', while there are examples from Kintyre and Bute. The reason would seem to be that Arran was occupied by the Vikings long enough for its Dalriadic rent place-names to fall into disuse. The pre-feudal rent place-names of Arran are such as Dippen, Pien, Penrioch, Penalister or Benalister, Aucheleffan, Levencorroch, and Feoline, which indicate that the farms or fields in question paid rent valued in multiples or fractions of a penny: the Gaelic for twopence being *da pheighinn*, for a penny *peighinn*, for a halfpenny *leath-pheiguinn*, and for a farthing *feoirlinn*. The penny in question was of silver, containing a twentieth of an ounce. It was first introduced into Scotland by the Vikings.

SOMERLED AND THE LORDS OF THE ISLES

THE VIKINGS had come at first as mere plunderers, with few or no womenfolk, and when they settled in a new territory they often selected mates from among their local female captives. The eventual result was to undermine their hold on their conquests, for in the former territory of Dalriada – in Norse terms the Sudreyar, or Southern Isles – there arose a mixed population deriving its language and traditions from its Gaelic-speaking mothers. By the twelfth century the name 'Scot' was being applied to the people of the new united kingdom of Picts, Scots, British and Angles, and the term 'Gael' to the original Scots of the former Dalriada. The term applied to the Vikings was *gaill*, 'strangers', and the new mixed race of the Sudreyar became known as the *gaill-Gaidheil*, 'stranger-Gaels', in English rendered Gall-Gael. They began their struggle for independence not only against the Viking rulers of Man and the Sudreyar, but against the new feudal kingdom of Scotland, which was anxious to wrest the Western Isles from the overlordship of Norway.

The first leader to emerge as a virtually independent ruler of the old Dalriadic territory, and soon to style himself Ri Innse-Gall, 'King of the Isles of the Strangers', was Somerled, a man of mixed Norwegian and Scottish descent, who had married Raghnildis, a daughter of Olaf, King of Man and the Sudreyar. Somerled led a naval expedition against Olaf's son Godred in 1156, when his galleys, traditionally more manoeuvrable because they adopted a hinged rudder, gained a famous victory. Some of his galleys were almost certainly from Arran. The old Dalriadic area was ceded to him,

Left: Kilbride cemetery above Lamlash

35

RANALD AND THE
CISTERCIANS

*Although the Stewarts ultimately
prevailed, Ranald MacSomerled did
not fail to leave his mark on Arran,
and it was a mark of his piety rather
than of his prowess in war. After the
death of his father he completed the
Cistercian abbey at Saddell in
Kintyre, and among the lands with
which he endowed it were twenty
merklands in the fertile strath of
Shiskine. Since this grant precedes
the incorporation of Arran into the
Scottish kingdom, which took place
three years after the battle of Largs
in 1263, it has a bearing on whether
the establishment of the medieval
monastery on Holy Isle was the
work of Ranald, or of his
descendant, 'Good John of Islay',
Lord of the Isles and recognised as
such by the Scottish king.*

Godrod retaining Man and the Hebrides north of Ardnamurchan. From that date until Norway sold the Western Isles to Scotland, Somerled's sea-kingdom was virtually independent, although nominally he and his successors were under the overlordship of Norway for their island territories, and of Scotland for their mainland territories.

Somerled's struggle for independence, and possibly for the acquisition of a more extensive kingdom, brought him into conflict with the Scottish king, Malcolm II, and in an expedition into the upper Clyde he was killed at Renfrew, in 1164, near what is now Glasgow airport. After his death he was succeeded by a son with a good Norse name, Rognvaldr, 'world-ruler', more commonly known as Reginald from the Latin version of his name. In Gaelic it was rendered Raghnall, anglicised as Ranald. Somerled's name was Norse, too – Sumarlidi, meaning 'summer-traveller', a reference to the season which the Vikings preferred for their raiding.

Ranald certainly claimed Arran and seems to have come into conflict with a younger brother, Angus, who lived in Bute. From another brother, Dugall are descended the MacDougalls of Lorne, while from Ranald, whose descendants maintained their grip on Kintyre and the Dalriadic islands, came the MacDonalds of the Isles, taking their clan name from Ranald's son Donald. At this time surnames as we understand them were unknown; Ranald was Ranald MacSomerled, or MacSorley, and his son was Donald MacRanald, but after Donald's son Angus, who was of course Angus MacDonald, all direct descendants were MacDonalds.

Another permanent surname originating at this time, which was to dominate Scottish and British history for several centuries, and was to figure along with that of MacDonald in the history of Arran, was Stewart. A granddaughter of the defeated Angus MacSomerled, known in folk poetry as Angus of Arran, married Alexander the *Hie Steuart* or High Steward of Scotland, a Norman who on the strength of this marriage claimed Bute and Arran for himself, and invaded them to enforce his claim. He was not unopposed. Ruari MacRanald, a brother of Donald, King of the Isles, claimed Bute and Arran also, and considered that under the Celtic law of tanistry by which inheritance was not by right to the eldest son, he had a better claim than Alexander.

As an important court official, Alexander had of course the backing of the Scottish king and in the end the Stewarts prevailed, to gain not only Bute and Arran but the kingdom of Scotland, and eventually Great Britain itself; but for a long time the struggle between the MacDonalds and the Stewarts in the south-west of Scotland was a source of disruption, and in standard histories the MacDonalds have come to be regarded as lawless rebels. It should be remembered that they held traditional Celtic, as opposed to Norman, ideals of political right, and if they had some of the piratical blood of the Vikings in their veins, so too had those who brought the feudal system to England, by way of Normandy, in 1066, and to Scotland, by invitation of David I, less than one hundred years later.

Shiskine church, dedicated to St Molas

Whilst administratively Arran was part of the Norse Sudreyar, it was in the episcopal see of Sudreyar and Man, nominally under the archbishopric of Trondheim. During Norse rule the old Celtic chapels in Arran may have fallen into disuse, as happened on other islands. It is therefore almost certain that with the grant of the Shiskine lands to Saddell would go responsibility for any Arran chapels. If Holy Isle had by this time become a place of pilgrimage, as is suggested by the names cut into the walls of the cave of St Molas, some of them stylistically earlier than the date of the battle of Largs, it is likely that a small hospice was established for the accommodation of pilgrims – and the collection of their offerings. On the other hand, 'Good John of Islay' was indeed granted Kintyre in 1377, and would therefore have acquired an interest in Saddell Abbey. But although the Shiskine lands were retained by Saddell Abbey until it fell into disuse towards the end of the fifteenth century, the rest of Arran was by 1377 in the possession of the Stewarts, and it is unlikely that John of Islay would have been allowed to establish a monastery on Holy Isle.

Overleaf: The String – from the top of the pass looking north

THE BATTLE OF LARGS

THE LAST OF THE VIKING names carved on the walls of the cave of St Molas on Holy Isle are Arran's only visible link with an event which practically settled the conflict between the Stewarts and the MacDonalds of the Isles as far as Arran was concerned. This was the battle of Largs. On a wider scale it settled the conflict between Norway and Scotland over the Norse claim to all the Western Isles of Scotland.

When Alexander II succeeded William the Lion as King of Scotland in 1214 he inherited a kingdom consolidated by the subjection of the mainland territories most resistant to feudal rule: Galloway in the south-west, a nest of Gall-Gael, and the far north, for a long time under the Vikings. He turned his attention now to the mainland holdings of the descendants of Somerled, and brought these under the feudal superiority of the Scottish crown. This was too much for Ospak, a son of Dugall MacSomerled, who preferred to be loyal to Norway rather than Scotland, probably because it was further away. He went to Norway and was despatched by King Hakon with a fleet, to restore Norwegian supremacy. Although he gained some support and succeeded in capturing Rothesay Castle in Bute after three days of hard fighting, he had to retreat, and then died of sickness. His fleet of about eighty ships, after wintering on the Isle of Man and raiding Kintyre, which was being encroached upon by the Stewarts, returned to Norway. Alexander II offered to buy the Western Isles from King Hakon, but the offer was refused, and Alexander collected a fleet to take them by force. He died, however, on the island of Kerrera in Oban Bay, in 1249.

Alexander III determined to finish the work his father had begun, and so alarmed Hakon that he levied all Norway for men, and took to sea with a fleet which by the time it reached Kintyre had more than one hundred and twenty ships. With Hakon were Magnus of Man, Angus of Islay, nominally King of the Isles but losing his grip on Kintyre and Arran, and other leading descendants of Somerled. The only exception was Ewan, now chief of the kindred of Dugall MacSomerled, who had once refused to break with Hakon to satisfy Alexander II. He now refused to break with Alexander III to satisfy Hakon. He either naively believed that having made a promise, even under duress, he ought to keep it, or he was trimming his sails to the wind.

If it was the latter he was shrewd. After harrying Kintyre, Hakon brought his fleet round the Mull of Kintyre and anchored in Lamlash Bay. Here he began to parley with messengers from Alexander III, who was willing to compound for possession of Arran, Bute and the Cumbraes, but Hakon would make no concessions. Some of the fleet moved up to Cumbraes, and negotiations dragged on. It was late in September, with the weather likely to break, and it became clear to Hakon that Alexander was playing for time. The truce was abandoned, and Hakon sent some ships up Loch Long which crossed over the narrow isthmus between Arrochar and Tarbert and raided on Loch Lomond, right into the heart of Lennox.

Then on Monday, 1 October 1263, with the main fleet lying at the Cumbraes, a storm began. By morning four of the ships, one of them laden with supplies, were stranded at Largs. Scots there started to loot the supply ship, but the wind slackened, Hakon was able to send reinforcements, and the Scots were forced to retire. On Wednesday the looting was renewed, Hakon himself landed with a force, and the supplies were being transferred into smaller ships when a Scottish army was sighted. The Norse *Saga of Hakon* suggests there were some eight hundred Norwegians on the beach, while the Scots were ten times as many, five hundred of them mounted.

There may have been some bias in the saga estimate, but it is likely that the Norwegians were outnumbered. After a battle which raged up and down the coast all day – perhaps a series of skirmishes would be a more accurate description – the Norwegians succeeded in getting into their ships and sailing away. On the Thursday they landed on the Clyde coast again, presumably under truce, to take away their dead, and on Friday, the storm having slackened, they returned to Lamlash, and for several days lay anchored there, wondering whether to winter in Ireland as they were invited to do, or return to Norway. Hakon was for remaining, but his men were against it, so he sailed for home.

Before doing so he made a distribution of the islands. Bute was given to a Ruari, not Ruari MacRanald but one who claimed descent from Angus MacSomerled, and so was a rival to the claims of Alexander the High Steward. Arran was given to Murchard or Margad, whose descent is uncertain, but whose name would appear to be derived from *murcadh*, 'see warrior' in which case he may well have been an ancestor of the Murchies, who survive in Arran, and Kintyre, to this day.

But these grants were made by Hakon when his power to support them was slipping away. He fell ill at Kirkwall in Orkney while on his way home, and died there on 13 December. Three years later, at the Treaty of Perth in 1266, his successor agreed to sell the Western Isles to Scotland for 4,000 marks plus an annual payment of 100 marks – the Norway Annual.

So the Norwegian occupation of Arran, which had begun with the grave-mound at the mouth of the Blairmore burn associated with the raid of AD797, was brought to its close when the great fleet of Hakon, which first anchored in Lamlash Bay in September of 1263, sailed out of it in October, having been defeated more by skilful diplomacy and bad weather than from lack of valour.

It was probably in September that certain of Hakon's men, passing the time at Lamlash while waiting for the outcome of negotiations, cut their names on the wall of the cave of St Molas. A few of the runes cut there belong to an earlier date, but that others were cut in 1263 is clear from one which reads: *Vigleikr stallari reist*, 'Vigleikr the king's marshal cut this'.

Chambered cairn, Kilmory

BUDDHISTS

In recent years Lamlash has recovered its close association with a monastic community, when a Tibetan Buddhist community bought it for £350,000, with a view to building a spiritual retreat for fifty monks and nuns, to be used also as a place of contemplation for all faiths. After many years in which even casual visits to Holy Isle were discouraged by its private owners, it now appears that once again access to the island will be possible, for visitors wishing to visit the cave where St Molas began the tradition of solitary contemplation which the Tibetan Lama found so appealing – he was quoted as saying that 'Holy Isle has a powerful aura of spiritual energy'. Generations of pilgrims would agree with him.

MUSTARDS AND JAMS

THE MODERN FACTORY operated by Arran Provisions Ltd stands at the foot of Monamore Glen, just north of Lamlash, beside the site of an old water-driven meal mill which survived until 1967 when it was demolished because it was unsafe. Arran Provisions is the most successful business on the island, and shows what can be done given imaginative marketing, a quality product, and financial support from development agencies. They started out with Arran mustard, which came in various exotic forms, but from 1986 expanded their range of products to include jams, jellies and preserves. Arran Provisions employs over fifty people – the exact number varies seasonally. The factory is near the junction of what is known as the 'Ross Road', which crosses the southern part of the island to the west coast near Lagg. There is a factory shop.

Holy Island from Kingscross Point

Arran Provisions, Lamlash

4 ISLAND VISITORS
Whiting Bay and Tourism

THE MOST SOUTHERLY of the three coastal resorts on the eastern side of Arran is Whiting Bay. Travelling south from Lamlash you pass the road to King's Cross, where archaeological sites range in date from an Iron Age dun to a Viking boat burial and a World War II gun emplacement. Whiting Bay has a sandy beach at Sandbraes on the north side of the village, while on the south side is a youth hostel and the start of the walk to Glenashdale Falls and the Giants' Graves – prehistoric burial cairns. There is also a playing field and swing park, an eighteen-hole golf course, and plenty of outdoor activities.

Originally just farmland belonging to one of many coastal farms, Whiting Bay grew throughout the nineteenth century as Clyde resorts became more and more popular with Glasgow day-trippers and tourists. It also developed as a small fishing port, with nine herring boats based there in the 1840s. In the same period there were twenty-three boats at Lamlash, nine at Brodick, eight at Corrie and twelve at Lochranza, with others spread along the west coast totalling about one hundred in all. By 1914 there was herring fishing only from Lochranza and Pirnmill, and by 1928 it was extinct.

STEAMERS AND PIERS

THE GROWTH OF TOURISM in Arran began with the invention of the steamboat. The pier at Brodick, the first of the steamboat piers to be built on the island, was completed in 1872. Previously passengers had been landed by rowing boat at small stone jetties, and this practice continued elsewhere on the island until parliamentary orders for further piers were obtained: for Lamlash in 1883, Lochranza in 1886, and Whiting Bay in 1897. It took a few years for these to be built, and the last of them, at Whiting Bay, was not in use until 1901.

The holiday trade in Arran soon became a most important factor in the island economy, especially during the summer season. At one time steamers called at all the island piers, but today the main line of communication is from Ardrossan to Brodick. The piers at Lamlash and Whiting Bay were closed in 1954 and 1957, partly because they had become too expensive

Near Lochranza

Left: Whiting Bay and Holy Island

to maintain, and partly because passengers could save time and shorten the sea trip, often quite rough in winter, by disembarking at Brodick and making their way to Lamlash and Whiting Bay by bus or car.

The first car ferries introduced to the Brodick service, the MV *Arran* in 1954 and the much larger MV *Glen Sannox* in 1957, were equipped with hydraulic lifts. Although these were a great improvement as a means of disembarking cars – which had been on a couple of rather springy planks – they were nevertheless slow when the state of the tide left a deep gap to be negotiated between the car-deck and pier levels. When loaded during busy periods with its full complement of forty cars the *Glen Sannox* could not keep to its time table, and long delays were experienced in which travellers had to wait in places with few amenities and exposed to inclement weather. That the island survived as a holiday resort was a great tribute to its popularity.

The arrival in 1970 of the stern-loading *Caledonia* ended these delays, but the new service was not without its teething troubles, for Ardrossan harbour is difficult to leave or enter in stormy weather. Caledonian MacBrayne was the company which under the Scottish Transport Group took over from the Caledonian Steam Packet Company in 1972, having converted the piers at Brodick and Ardrossan to meet the needs of the new stern-loading vessels. But if the *Caledonia* was unable to make Ardrossan harbour it had to sail to Gourock, the nearest alternative harbour suitably equipped. This more than doubled the sea voyage, and passengers awaiting at Ardrossan to embark when the boat arrived from Brodick had to be taken from Ardrossan to Brodick by bus, a distance of some thirty miles (48km). Fortunately for visitors these experiences were less frequent in summer than in winter, but in winter they occurred too often. Many islanders sighed for the good old days when the boat could use the now abandoned Fairlie Pier, not far up the coast, when Ardrossan was stormbound.

The *Caledonia* was followed by the *Clansman*, also stern-loading, which could carry 876 passengers and 55 cars, as against the 650 passengers and 40 cars of its predecessor. The *Clansman*, an old boat adapted for the Arran run, was in turn superseded in 1984 by the *Isle of Arran*, and able to take 850 passengers and 75 cars. Although the Ardrossan – Brodick service has five or six round trips on weekdays and three or four on Sundays during the summer season, it is usually very busy and booking for both vehicles and passengers is recommended. In winter a greatly reduced service operates. For the latest information on ferry services contact Caledonian MacBrayne (tel Ardrossan (01294) 463470 or Brodick (01770) 302166). The ferry company has a 'Day Saver' scheme with reduced rates for a car and four passengers, and also an 'Island Hopscotch' scheme – for example, visitors may decide to continue their trip by way of the Lochranza – Claonaig route to Kintyre, connecting to Islay, Jura and Colonsay.

Until about 1930, horse wagonettes still met the steamboats at the piers, although the first motor car had come to the island, on the PS *Jupiter*,

ISLAND TRANSPORT

The earliest visitors of the railway and steamboat era, such as Lord Cockburn, had to make their expeditions into Glen Rosa and Glen Sannox either on foot or horseback, but wheeled transport arrived in 1863. In the early 1800s farms were very small, their boundaries established by the divisions planned in 1814; then came a period of amalgamation, and in the 1860s one MacBride lost his land when Peter MacDonald, lessee of the Douglas Hotel, became tenant of the new enlarged farm of Brandon Bank, and combined farming with his innkeeping. Reduced to the status of a cottar, MacBride imported a wagon from the mainland and ran it for hire. It was the first spring vehicle to be seen in Arran, but was unfortunately lost at sea when being taken to Irvine for repair. Later in the century its journey would have been unnecessary for by then there was at least one family of coachbuilders on the island, the Mackenzies of Shiskine, whose vans were beautiful pieces of craftsmanship; some of these would have been seen lurking behind more modern vehicles in the Victorian premises of certain of the island's butchers and grocers, until they were bought up by collectors.

Left: The paddle steamer Waverley *leaving Brodick pier as the modern car ferry arrives (C. Currie)*

as early as 1897 and caused a sensation by travelling from Brodick to Sannox, a distance of seven miles (11km), in thirty-five minutes. The first bus on the island was bought from the Albion works by Colin Currie of Balmichael, who had carried mail, goods and passengers to the west of the island throughout the days of wheeled horse transport. Asked cautiously about payment, he drew the necessary cash from his pocket. Further bus enterprises developed along mail routes served by Ernest Ribbeck and Donald Stewart to the north and south-west respectively. Ernest Ribbeck was one of two brothers, saddlers by trade, who had come to Brodick in the days of Princess Marie of Baden and were favoured because of their nationality; Ernest became postmaster at Brodick in 1871. He brought a horse vehicle into service and took over the delivery of mail from Brodick to the post office at Corrie from Robert Douglas, the postmaster there, who had previously made the journey on foot. Ernest's daughter followed him in Brodick post office, which in 1913 was moved to the building which later became Pelligrini's café. His son Kaspar followed him on the Corrie mail route. In the 1920s Kaspar developed a bus service on the Corrie route, and this initiated a burst of enterprise which was to reach its peak in 1962 when seven bus companies operated, from Brodick, Lamlash, Whiting Bay, Kildonan, Blackwaterfoot, Machrie and Pirnmill.

Kilpatrick

Public transport has shrunk since that time, as the advent of car ferries led to a rapid increase in the number of motor vehicles on the island: the increase in the number of island car owners, and the number of holiday visitors who brought their own cars, led to a drastic reduction in the numbers making use of the buses. By 1967, bus services in winter had been reduced to fewer than might reasonably be considered even a skeleton service. In recent years, however, the situation has improved, and certainly in summer public transport is excellent, with buses meeting most sailings to and from Brodick and Lochranza, and many excursion tours available. In addition, many of the hotels and outdoor centres operate minibuses for the benefit of their customers.

The earliest promotion of Arran as a destination for tourists came in 1828, when the Reverend Dr David Landsborough published his *Arran, a Poem in Six Cantos*, a work written in a style reminiscent of Wordsworth, another poet associated with the fashion for scenery. In 1847 the same author published a book of prose, *Excursions in Arran, with reference to the Natural History of the Island*, with a reprint of his earlier poem added. This edition proved popular, and another series of *Excursions* followed in 1852. His son continued these literary efforts, and in 1873 a volume was published

Previous page: Glen Shurig

containing edited extracts from his father's writing, with a memoir and other chapters of a miscellaneous character written by himself. These constitute the earliest works classing as tourist literature concerning the island; they were added to in the nineteenth century only by George Milner, who in 1894 published *Studies of Nature on the Coast of Arran*, and this in spite of its title is simply a delightful account of a summer holiday spent at Corrie.

To the Landsboroughs, therefore, is due almost sole credit for providing Arran visitors, in the developing years of the island's holiday trade, with something useful to read, either in anticipation of their visit, or while confined to their lodgings by inclement weather. Today, however, the *Excursions* are in parts almost unreadable, largely because of wearisome repetition in the botanical lists and also because of a compulsion to grasp every possible excuse for the preaching of a sermon. Yet we must admire the two men because in spite of their pedantry and fervour, they were men of vigour. They established a fashion for strenuous open-air holidays still followed by many regular visitors to Arran, their activities including scrambles to the summits of the northern peaks, expeditions to the most remote lochs, picnics in the glens, usually beside the larger pools where a bathe was possible, and inshore fishing in the evenings from sailing or rowing boats. The island will never have anything better to offer.

Although the Rev Landsborough senior was qualified to discourse on the natural history of Arran, he also took pains to learn what he could about its human past. Unfortunately much of his historical information is inaccurate, made worse by a tendency to indulge in the imaginative reconstruction of any scenes which he thought picturesque to the extent that history was drowned in fiction. Nevertheless, these early efforts helped to attract others to the island who could investigate its archaeology and history with greater prospect of success, and for this the Landsboroughs deserve our gratitude.

Partly because they were unable to communicate with the islanders in their own language, and partly because they identified themselves with the gentry, the Landsboroughs tell us little of how the local people lived. The father did refer back to the year 1841: this was some twelve years after the Sannox clearances, when elderly people had lost access to land but had not left the island, and were lingering on in poverty in decaying old black-houses – he described these as being the poorest dwellings he had seen inhabited by human beings. There were a few slightly more complimentary references, as that to the little inn at Urinbeg, Lochranza, run by a Mrs MacLarty who 'notwithstanding her inauspicious name, was kind and cleanly, and did everything in her power to render us comfortable' (for the benefit of non-Scottish readers it should be explained that 'clartie' is Scots for 'dirty'). They do give us a few glimpses of island life out-of-doors, too, of open-air services and communions, and the bustle of the fishing community on the Lochranza shore; but essentially the Landsboroughs remain onlookers, cut off from the people by barriers of race, language and class.

5 FACING SOUTH TO PLADDA
The Southern Coast from Kildonan to Sliddery

Kildonan Castle

THE SOUTHERN PART of Arran represents the Lowland of this 'Scotland in miniature', distinguished by its fertility and low, rounded hills from the harsher landscapes north of the String Road. There are excellent views down the Firth of Clyde to the Ayrshire coast, Ailsa Craig, Pladda and, as you turn the south-west corner of Arran, to Kintyre.

On the south-east corner of the island there is a small loop of road leading to Kildonan where there is an excellent sandy beach, a prehistoric fort, an Early Christian chapel site and a castle. The medium-sized Iron Age fort at Kildonan is poorly preserved, and of Kildonan Castle only a fragment of walling remains. It was a tower house originally, but although it may look picturesque now it is actually in a highly dangerous state. Almost nothing is known of its owners, or of when it was built, but for much of its life it was a stronghold of the Stewarts. In 1549, when Dean Monro visited the island, it was in the possession of James Stewart, Sheriff of Bute.

Kildonan takes its name from St Donan, another Irish monk who maintained a cell or *cill* there in the sixth century AD. The 'kil' prefix in a place-name usually indicates an Early Christian monastic site: others in Arran can be found at Kilpatrick, Kilmory, Kilbride Bennan, Kilbride at Lamlash, and Kilmichael at Brodick. Other Christian sites are at St Michael's Chapel at Sannox, St James's at Lochranza, St Mary's at Sliddery and at the chapel dedicated to St Blaise on Pladda. We have already discussed St Molas of Holy Isle.

Kilmory and Glen Ree indicate that this church site is dedicated to St Maolrubha, more usually associated with the monastery at Applecross in Wester Ross, which he founded. On the other hand, there are dedications to him in Kintyre and Islay (Kilarrow). Many of these Early Christian missionary-monks seem to have journeyed extensively throughout what was then Pictland, making converts and establishing new monasteries and chapels as they went.

PARISH EDUCATION

IN 1698 an act of Parliament made it compulsory for heritors or landowners to establish and maintain a school in every parish; they were allowed to make their tenants pay half the *stent* or rate agreed for this purpose. Neither landowners nor tenants were anxious to assume the burden, in spite of the misappropriated church lands from which many of the former drew revenue, and as the kirk sessions responsible for administering the schools had no way of forcing them to do so, except by moral persuasion, it was almost a century after the passing of the act before John Knox's ideal of a school in every parish was realised. The position in Arran does not seem to have been as bad as in some other parts of Scotland.

For example, in the records of 1704 for Kilmory parish there is an entry concerning the construction of a school building, ordered at a cost of 40 Scottish pounds, to be paid for out of *mulcts* or fines imposed upon certain types of offender for breaches of moral law. It was to be a simple building of stone and clay, 'without divot except one going or two upon the top of the wall thereof', 42 feet long by 13 feet broad (12.8 by 3.96m), with three gables and two doors; which suggests that it was to be in two parts, one the schoolroom and the other a single-roomed dwelling for the schoolmaster. 'Sufficient lights' were stipulated, which probably meant there would be unglazed windows on opposite sides of each apartment, with shutters which would be manipulated according to the direction of the weather, as in the local black-houses. Like them, the school building would be thatched with divot and heather, and would have its hearth on the floor. There appear to have been similar schools at Kilbride, in the Blairmore area beside the old church of St Brigid, and also in the Glenashdale district.

Matters were improved by an act of 1803 which made provision for

BARNS, CAVES, PEAT AND A DRAM

As well as these schools there seem to have been others, conducted in schoolmasters' houses or in barns or caves, financed partly by the kirk sessions, partly by the parents, and partly from the fees paid for each subject taught. Besides paying fees the children took peats to school in winter for the fire, and on St Bride's day, 1 February, they brought presents of money to the schoolmaster, the boy and girl giving the largest amounts being crowned king and queen for the day with paper crowns; they then all marched off, sustained by a dram of toddy supplied by the schoolmaster, for a holiday.

Torr A' Chaistel – two miles west of Kilmory

'side schools' in those parts of a parish too remote to be served by the main parochial schools; it also laid down maximum and minimum salaries for the principal schoolmasters, to be paid by the landowners and tenants, who besides the salaries had to supply – for the principal schoolmasters only – a house of not more than two rooms. There was talk at the time of 'places for dominies' (the Scots word for a rural schoolmaster). The act therefore gave recognition to the side schools already in existence, making them a proper charge on landowners and tenants.

Accommodation does not seem to have improved immediately, for there is a record as late as 1845 of an accident in a side school at Feorline, where the walls of a potato barn being used as a schoolroom fell during the thaw following a severe frost, crushing five little girls to death. This tragedy seems happily to have been an isolated circumstance, and by the time it happened Arran had no fewer than eight parochial schools, four in each of the two parishes, Kilbride and Kilmory.

It appears that the salaries of the eight parochial schoolmasters were met in each parish by dividing among them, in proportion to the number of their pupils, a single maximum salary. Thus in Kilbride parish the salaries were for Lamlash £19, Brodick £16, Corrie £4, and Lochranza £6, although this last was a joint school with Kilmory, from which the schoolmaster had a further payment . At about the same time the salaries for Kilmory parish were for Kilmory £17 10s, Shiskine £15, Imachar £5 16s and Lochranza £10 10s, the

Kilmory church

last again only a part payment. All the parochial schoolmasters on the island, except at Imachar, had a free house with garden and 'glebe'. By this time the main schoolhouses, although still thatched, were built of stone and lime, had chimneys in the gables, and were whitewashed. In both parishes, as in other parts of Scotland, children still paid fees, those for Kilmory being for reading 2s, for reading and writing 2s 6d, for these plus arithmetic 3s, or Latin 5s, all per quarter. Book-keeping and navigation cost respectively £1 and £1 10s. It was stipulated that all teachers in the parish should be able to teach Gaelic, which of course was necessary for the teaching of English.

It seems that the largest school on the island could draw no more from fees than £14 a year, and the smallest not more than £5, which even if we assume that the fees went to the schoolmaster in addition to his salary, means that most were little better off than farm servants, and worse off then skilled workmen such as masons or carpenters; for in 1840 the former earned from £6 to £8 in the half year, and the latter from 3s to 3s 6d a day. Each of the parish ministers had a free manse and glebe and more than three times the income of the best paid teachers.

Generous as the provision of parochial schools was, as compared with that in many other parts of Scotland, it was insufficient for the needs of an island with such scattered communities, and in addition to its four parochial schools Kilbride had at least two others, one at Whiting Bay set up by the General Assembly, and the other a private school in Lamlash, maintained at

the expense of the parents. Kilmory was still the more populous parish even in the 1840s, and had in addition to its four parochial schools eight others, two of them set up by the General Assembly, and six private. After the Disruption of 1843 the Free Church established its own school at Balmichael, a successor to that conducted in the cave at Kilpatrick, in the earlier days of the patronage disputes.

The system remained unchanged until the passing of the Scottish Education Act of 1872, but before that date, the building of greatly improved schoolhouses accompanied that of such estate housing enterprises in Brodick as Alma Terrace and Douglas Row. The red sandstone Victorian schoolhouse is a fair sample of the improved schools built by the 11th Duke of Hamilton; it was opened in 1856.

The Scottish Education Act of 1872 set up the Scottish Education Department and made education compulsory for all children between the ages of five and thirteen; the administration of the schools was taken out of the hands of the kirk sessions and made the responsibility of school boards elected by the rate payers of each parish. Fees were still charged, but those unable to pay were given assistance from the rates. Schools became subject to government inspection, and grants were paid if the pupils reached a prescribed standard. In 1883 the school leaving age was raised to fourteen, where it was to remain for another sixty-three years. In 1888 the leaving certificate examination, which was to become accepted as the gateway to the universities, was established. In 1891 fees for children between the ages of five and fourteen were abolished.

The Victorian school buildings still stand at Kildonan, Kilmory, Sliddery, Shiskine, Machrie, Pirnmill, Lochranza, Corrie, Brodick and Lamlash, though most are used now for other purposes.

EARLY FARMING LIFE

AT THE BEGINNING of the nineteenth century agriculture in Arran was reorganised, that is to say, smallholdings were eliminated and amalgamated into more economic units as part of the introduction of sheep farming. Before this, most Arran folk lived in farming settlements known as *clachans*, operating a communal farming system. The modern villages of Lochranza, Corrie, Brodick, Lamlash, Whiting Bay, Kildonan, Kilmory, Blackwaterfoot and Pirnmill did not then exist.

These *clachans* were compact clusters of long black-houses and their outbuildings, consisting of stables and barns. The black-houses were built of double courses of dry stone, rubble-cored, and plastered on the inside with clay. They were thatched with heather, or less frequently straw, laid over turves resting on brushwood; this in turn rested on horizontal poles fastened to the roof couplings, all the timber being undressed. The houses were divided into three compartments: an inner room, a kitchen, and a byre for

Previous page: The view from near Dun Kilpatrick, looking to the hills in the north-west of the island

cattle. The kitchen had two windows, unglazed but shuttered, which faced back and front so that one or other could be opened, according to the direction of the weather, to provide light. The kitchen hearth was on the floor, usually near the middle. From a rafter above this hung a *swee*, or swinging metal arm to hold cooking pots, and into the roof directly above was built a plastered wicker chimney, hooded against the prevailing wind. The kitchen was divided from the inner room by two box-beds, one usually facing into the kitchen itself, and the other into the inner room. The doorway into the inner room occupied the space between them.

The inner room sometimes had a wooden floor, and the rafters above it were usually covered with boarding to form a garret above. The window of the inner room was sometimes glazed, and there might be a fireplace and chimney built into the gable. The rafters above the kitchen were not boarded over, but a ladder from the kitchen gave access to the garret above the inner room, which was usually a sleeping place for children.

The kitchen floor was composed of a mixture of ashes, clay and lime, beaten until it was compact. Between the kitchen and the byre there was a wicker partition, hardly enough to reach to the rafters. The doorway to the kitchen from the open air was usually closed to this partition, and was itself protected by a wicker screen. There was of course a doorway through the partition into the byre, and at the far end of the latter, in the gable, there was a second doorway for the cattle.

Clauchen Glen preaching house and cemetery

ARABLE SYSTEMS

The arable ground closest to each community, the infield, was cultivated year after year and manured regularly with animal dung, seaweed and shell sand. The outlying arable ground, or outfield, was cultivated originally on a three-plot system, cropping one year, lying fallow the next, and on the third being grazed, and of course dunged, by the farm animals. The crops grown were oats, barley, peas and beans. Potatoes came into use at the start of the nineteenth century, and were soon as important as oats, with flax also grown.

59

Sometimes both cattle and horses, the latter small garrons, occupied the byre end of the house, although usually the horses seem to have been housed separately, in small stables sometimes built onto the outside of the inner room gable but more often detached. Grain was threshed by hand in little barns which had doors opposite each other so that a draught was provided when they were opened, to blow away the chaff. The grain was dried in kilns, over straw placed on slats above a hearth, and ground in one of the estate mills to which the farms were thirled, although small quantities were sometimes ground by hand using the quern stones still to be seen by the doorways of the older cottages. In each *clachan* were a few enclosures where animals could be penned, and from these a track led out to the hill pastures.

The animals kept were mainly little black milk cows and their followers, with fine-woolled native sheep to about half the number of the cattle, and horses to about a third. There were some goats, but only a few pigs. Cattle and horses were the chief exports. Sheep and goats were killed at Michaelmas and the meat either dried for winter provision, or sold at Greenock. Some salt butter was also sold on the mainland, as were herring nets and thread made from the island flax, and there was a herring fishery.

The inhabitants' diet consisted of meal, potatoes, butter, cheese and eggs, with dried mutton and goat, and salt herrings in the winter. It appears that very little beef was eaten: the cattle were probably much too precious to be killed for home consumption, at least by the poorer people. The men spent the spring labouring on the land, the summer cutting peat and doing building repairs, the period before and after harvest fishing and burning kelp, and the winter making herring nets. The women set the potatoes, made butter and cheese, helped at the harvest and when seaweed was gathered for kelp, and dressed and spun the flax and wool to be made into clothing for their families by the handloom weavers in the larger *clachans*, and the travelling tailors. Much of the butter was salted for sale on the mainland and was made by the younger women at the *sheilings*, turf shelters up in the hills where the cattle were shifted in summer to take advantage of the seasonal flush of grass; this practice was also to let the meadows grow to hay, and to allow the pastures on the plots of outfield to lie fallow and so rest.

The people of each *clachan* worked as a community, and tasks were allocated amongst its members by the *fear a bhaile* or 'man of the village'; this individual was usually also the tacksman whose task it was to collect an annual rent from each family, and who paid an annual rent himself to the estate. The rent to be paid by each family to the tacksman was at first determined by its wealth in cattle. The hill pasture was held in common by the members of the *clachan* community and was *soumed*, each family having so many *soums*. A *soum* being an amount sufficient for the grazing of one cow or six sheep, or half the grazing for a horse. Each family's allocation of arable ground and of the meadows corresponded in turn to its share in the *souming*, although these shares were spread over the ground in a manner determined annually by lot.

Previous page: Glen Rosa with Beinn Nuis on the left

The ground to be cultivated in any one year was organised in several plots of varying sizes, determined largely by the lie of the ground; each was separated from the other by the fallow of previous years, or by a rocky outcrop, a steep slope, a stretch of bog or a burn. In each of these plots there would be so many 'rigs', and it seems to have been in terms of rigs and their constituent furrows that each plot was divided among the sub-tenants.

In true *runrig* system the allocation was made annually, and the labour of the community applied to the farm as a whole. It was in some ways a primitive system of agriculture, and inefficient, involving as it did scattered holdings. However, agricultural knowledge grew rapidly from the middle of the eighteenth to the middle of the nineteenth centuries, and there were many useful discoveries in respect of drainage, liming and crop rotation, and the introduction of new crops, the improvement of implements, and the selective breeding of animals. Unfortunately some of the new ideas, which were often espoused enthusiastically by Scottish lairds, were to prove unsuitable in Scotland's climate, and others were miscalculated in their long-term effects. And even those which were to prove effective were introduced to the runrig areas in such a way that technical progress was achieved at the expense of social justice.

In Arran, plans for change were put in hand in 1766: Douglas the 7th Duke of Hamilton was a minor, and the trustees of the estate commissioned John Burrel to come to the island and make plans for introducing the new style of farming. In 1773 Burrel submitted his proposals. He noted that the 99 farms of the estate maintained 1,110 families, an average of about 10 families to each farm, and put forward a system which would reduce the number of families to 250, with the heads of these families paying rent direct to the estate, to whom the new holdings were to be leased. So some 750 heads of families would have been deprived of access to land, and consequently at that time almost inevitably of the possibility of providing for themselves and their children, except as casual labourers employed by those more fortunate than themselves in obtaining leases. There was only one solution to Burrel's proposals – massive emigration and depopulation of the island. This is the process known throughout the Highlands as the Clearances.

We close this chapter with a table giving the population figures for Arran's two parishes in the decennial official census records from 1801 to 1981. Two important statistics stand out: in the century from a peak of 6,541 in 1821, the population of Arran dropped by around 2,000; and there was very nearly a catastrophic drop in the population in the 1950s and 1960s – at one time a drop of 20 per cent in ten years. If that trend had continued the population by 1981 would have dropped to just over 2,000. That this did not happen was due to a combination of changing social trends and some judicious social engineering. Disguised in the parish breakdown is another important trend – that Arran's indigenous population is concentrated in the eastern part of the island.

POPULATION TABLE

	Kilbride Parish	Kilmory Parish	Arran
1801	2,183	2,996	5,179
1811	2,274	3,430	5,704
1821	2,714	3,827	6,541
1831	2,656	3,771	6,427
1841	2,786	3,455	6,241
1851	2,512	3,414	5,926
1861	2,408	3,148	5,556
1871	2,290	2,778	5,068
1881	2,153	2,580	4,733
1891	2,298	2,482	4,780
1901	2,469	2,297	4,766
1911	2,451	2,177	4,628
1931	2,685	1,874	4,532
1941	2,800	1,750	4,550 (est)
1951	3,158	1,498	4,656
1961	2,532	1,181	3,577
1971	2,243	1,196	3,569
1981	3,238	1,505	4,743

Overleaf: Glenashdale Falls

6 SPIDERS AND STANDING STONES
Blackwaterfoot, Shiskine and Machrie Moor

THE COAST ROAD winds its way round the bottom left-hand corner of Arran and turns north, meandering through farming scenery past Corriecravie to Blackwaterfoot. This is a beautiful little village with a tiny harbour at the point where the Blackwaterfoot burn flows into the sea. Beside the sea is a twelve-hole golf course, overlooking a long sandy beach. The village has hotels, shops, an all-year-round bowling green, tennis courts and a putting green.

Inland from Blackwaterfoot is the fertile Shiskine valley: the small villages of Shiskine and Ballymichael are situated on the western side of the String Road which heads across the middle of Arran to Brodick. Near Blackwaterfoot are two areas of outstanding interest: Drumadoon Point lying to the west, with the King's Cave where Robert the Bruce reputedly gained encouragement from a spider; while 3 miles (5km) to the north is Machrie Moor, with an outstanding complex of prehistoric standing stones and stone circles.

DRUMADOON

DRUMADOON POINT has something for everybody: long coastal walks, dramatic cliff scenery, interesting birds and flowers, a prehistoric fort and excellent geology. It is reached either by the shore or from the golf course at Blackwaterfoot. The headland of Drumadoon (meaning 'ridge of the fort') is a spectacular columnar basalt cliff. The fairly level hilltop area of about twelve acres (4.8 hectares) is defended on the west or seaward side by perpendicular cliffs, and on the east or landward side, and at its northern and southern ends, by a crescent-shaped wall of stone, possibly originally about 10 feet (3m) thick but so depleted that its original height cannot be estimated. It is by far the largest of the Iron Age forts on Arran, and for that reason is regarded as the tribal stronghold for the island's chief, capable in times of trouble of defending most of the Iron Age population of the island against invaders. More cynically, perhaps the large size was needed to accommodate the tribal chieftain's cattle, which were the major source of his wealth, power and prestige.

JAMES AND THOMAS BRYCE

There are the remains of ten stone circles on Arran, of which seven are near Machrie. All received the attention of early travellers to the island, who recorded the local tradition that they were connected with the legendary Fionn and his warriors. James Bryce – who also wrote a work on the geology of the island – surveyed them in 1861, though not very accurately, and left records used by Thomas Bryce in his own survey for the first volume of The Book of Arran. James Bryce found burials within several of the circles and therefore concluded that their purpose was sepulchral, and Thomas Bryce seems to have agreed. However, most modern archaeologists would dissent from this view.

Top left: Blackwaterfoot from near Dun Kilpatrick

Bottom left: Shiskine golf course from the Doon

THE KING'S CAVE

The historical association of the King's Cave at Drumadoon with Robert the Bruce has already been discussed (see p25) and dismissed for lack of evidence as unlikely, to say the least. The island of Rathlin, off the coast of Northern Ireland, seems to have a far better claim to Bruce's spider. However, this does not stop hoards of visitors making the pilgrimage to the King's Cave, although most do not linger long because of the rather unpleasant musty smell. The tradition is not very old – both Martin Martin (1695) and Pennant (1772) refer to associations with Fionn, the hero of Irish folklore, without mentioning Bruce at all – and one suspects the creative imagination of Victorian antiquarians, or Victorian hoteliers.

Top right: Drumadoon Point from the north

Bottom right: The Doon

We know little enough about these Iron Age folk. They probably arrived on Arran around 800 – 900BC and built hill top forts, some of which are 'vitrified' – a hard, glassy effect caused by rock melting at very high temperatures, seen on Arran at the cliff top fort at Sannox. Drumadoon may date from around 500BC, but in the absence of excavation exact dating is impossible. Later in the Iron Age, presumably in conditions of improved security, the leading families in each locality began to build their own, family-sized fortification, known as a 'dun' (pronounced 'doon') from the Gaelic word for fort.

During the Roman occupation of Scotland a naval expedition sailed round the Scottish coasts, and as a result of intelligence gathered from that expedition the Alexandrian geographer Ptolemy, working in the second century AD, prepared a map which included the names of the Iron Age tribes encountered by the Romans. Ptolemy's map clearly indicates that Kintyre and Islay were inhabited by the Epidii – their name suggests that they spoke a Celtic language represented today by Welsh, Cornish and Breton, rather than that spoken by the Dalriadic Scots, represented today by Irish, Manx and Scots Gaelic. Epidii means 'the portion of the horse people', the suffix being Latin but the first element, *ep*, meaning 'horse' (cognate with the Latin *equus*, and the Gaelic *each* or *ech*). The surname MacEachran, with numerous variations in spelling, means 'son of the horse lord' and is still a common family name in Argyll. It is possible that the Epidii inhabited Arran too. In view of the fact that Roman supply ships must have travelled regularly up the Clyde to their bases at Dumbarton and Erskine, it is very likely that the Romans at least scouted around the eastern coastline of Arran – but if they did so, no traces survive.

Needless to say, the views from the heights of Drumadoon are the best on the west side of Arran: across Kilbrannon Sound the whole length of the Kintyre peninsula can be seen, with the full expanse of the Firth of Clyde opening up to the south, and the rugged hills at the other end of Arran, to the north.

At the bottom of the spectacular cliffs at Drumadoon are caves eroded from the old red sandstone at the end of the last Ice Age, formed when the sea level was higher during the time of the 25 foot (7.6m) raised beach. On the central pillar of the cave now known as the King's Cave are carvings which are probably Early Christian in date: there is a cross, rising out of stylised foliage; and to its right, the upper half of a human figure with both arms raised, and in the hands what appears to be a bow, held in such a way as to form an arc over the head. Some writers see a similarity between these, and also two carvings of horses, with carvings on Pictish stones in northern Scotland; others have suggested a Viking presence. Unfortunately the ones here are very difficult to make out, the result of vandalism, and the increasing ravages of time and a polluted environment; although we do have drawings in the 1910 *Book of Arran* to refer to for assistance. In view of the Christian cross it is not unreasonable to suppose that the 'King's Cave' was occupied at about the same time as the cave on Holy Isle, on the other side of Arran.

Auchagallon stone circle

MACHRIE MOOR

TO THE NORTH of Blackwaterfoot is an equally interesting landscape, with an equally obscure history. The Bronze Age ritual landscape of Machrie Moor is likely to have been in use in the second millennium BC, abandoned perhaps soon after 1200BC in a period of deteriorating climate.

Access to the standing stones and stone circles of Machrie is by way of an easy walk across moorland, over well-marked paths. There are information panels to explain the monuments, although no words are needed to convey the impression of mystery and power which was surely intended by the builders. However, all ideas and theories about their use must, of necessity, remain speculative. Perhaps the most intriguing is that they have some kind of ceremonial function linked to astronomical observations of the complicated movements of sun, moon and stars.

The first stone circle encountered on Machrie Moor lies about halfway between the public road and Moss Farm; it was described in 1862 as a huge

Left: Shiskine golf course and the Doon

71

circle over 62 feet (19m) in diameter, made up of granite blocks standing 3 feet (almost 1m) high. It was probably not a true stone circle, and the granite blocks were more likely to be the kerbstones of a huge round cairn of small stones, later quarried away. Just beside Moss Farm is a complex circle consisting of two concentric rings of stones: the inner ring consists of eight round-topped granite blocks, with an outer circle of fifteen slightly smaller stones. James Bryce found a previously disturbed burial cist in the centre.

About a hundred yards (91m) to the east is a 'four-poster': four stones aligned on the points of the compass. To its north is an oval ring of six roughly dressed slabs of old red sandstone, of which only one is upright. About a hundred yards (91m) to the east of the sandstone ring is the site most visitors will recognise from picture postcards and tourist brochures, or from the front cover of the excellent Historic Scotland guidebook, *The Ancient Monuments of Arran*: three massive sandstone pillars which are still upright, and another four or five which have fallen; the tallest is some 18 feet (5.5m) high. In 1861 James Bryce found two burials inside the circle, in one of which was a typical Bronze Age pottery vessel known as a food vessel, beautifully decorated with incised bands. The diameter of this circle is 42 feet (12.8m).

To the east of this much-photographed site are two other circles. The smaller of the two lies about 233 yards (213m) east of Moss Farm and consists of eleven stones, made of alternating granite boulders and sandstone slabs. Excavations in 1985 showed that an earlier timber circle stood on the same site.

To the north is another circle, unknown until discovered by probing the overlying peat in 1975. It was excavated in 1985 and 1986, and found to consist of ten stones, nine of granite and one of sandstone, the tallest just over 3 feet (1m) high. Traces of a timber circle were found here, too, probably of an earlier date than the stones.

Machrie Moor is a surviving Bronze Age landscape of outstanding importance, still largely covered by peat. All around are cairns, standing stones and hut circles; some of the cairns are Neolithic, dating to before 3000BC. The whole area must have been used for rituals and ceremonies for almost two thousand years. Furthermore, as well as the ceremonial sites, there are many indications of a cultivated and farmed landscape, with field boundaries and stock enclosures, and evidence of Bronze Age houses.

Comparisons have been drawn with the Kilmartin river valley on the mainland of Argyll north of Lochgilphead, and not very far by sea from Machrie Moor. There, the close proximity of copper ores caused prehistorians to wonder if that was a factor in the creation of another ritual landscape, with standing stones, cairns in a linear cemetery extending over several miles, and a stone circle at Temple Wood. Despite much research and excavation in recent years, our understanding of the culture and society of the Bronze Age is still a mixture of speculation and educated probabilities, and much remains to be done.

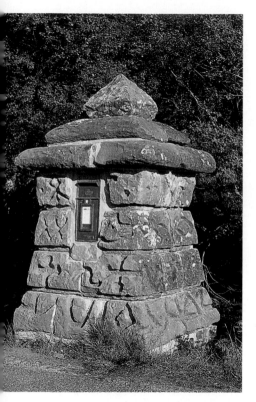

On the String Road by the junction with Machrie Road

Right: Raised beach at Imachar Point

7 Kintyre & the Twelve Apostles
The West Coast from Pirnmill to Catacol

THE ROAD NORTH from Machrie passes through the small coastal settlements of Dougrie, Balliekine and Imachar, rounds Whitefarland Point, and then comes to the lovely little village of Pirnmill. The lands of Dougarre, previously rented to Ranald MacAlister, were granted to Alexander Montgomery, Lord Skelmorlie, ancestor of the Earls of Eglinton, along with the lands of 'Kendloch of Ransay, Cathaydill, the two Turreguys, Alltgoulach, Auchegallane, Tymoquhare, and Penreoch' – all in this part of Arran. This was in 1452.

Dougrie Lodge was built as a shooting lodge in the last half of the nineteenth century. Grouse shooting and deer stalking became extremely popular after Queen Victoria had initiated the custom of royal holidays at Balmoral, from 1849. In Arran, the north end of the island was developed as deer forest, and much of the rest of the interior as grouse moor. Balliekine is the Arran terminus of the power cable which brings electricity from the mainland, from across Kilbrannan Sound at Carradale. In the 1970s, private forestry plantations on the estate heralded a period of tree-planting in other parts of Arran, too.

Pirnmill

Pirnmill takes its name from a type of bobbin used in the cotton industry; with the growth in the production of cotton on the mainland, a mill for the manufacture of bobbins was established here. The village was also a small centre for herring fishing up until the 1920s. North of Pirnmill, at Mid Thunderguy, a path leads up into the hills to one of Arran's most accessible hill lochs, Coire an Lochan.

Twelve Apostles, Catacol

EMIGRATIONS

THE TWELVE APOSTLES

The village of Catacol is well known for its twelve almost identical cottages, known as the 'Twelve Apostles'. Attractive as they are, they are evidence of a sad episode in Arran's history, as they were built in 1863 to house islanders cleared from Glen Catacol in favour of deer, which at the time were more profitable than sheep. By this time most of the Arran glens had already been cleared, and many islanders had joined the emigrations to North America.

Right: Glen Catacol

THE ABOLITION of communal farms and the great increase in the number of small coastal holdings and in the number of families thus able to make a living from the combination of the potato, kelp and fishing, had already absorbed all the displaced persons it could, when the creation of extensive sheep farms was planned for the larger glens at the close of the leases initiated in 1814. The introduction of sheep involved even more displacement, and it happened at the same time as the kelp industry collapsed, the end of the Napoleonic wars having restored the trade in Spanish barilla, an easier and cheaper alternative.

At the close of the American wars Canada was being developed as a British colony, and this provided a destination for emigrants. The fashion for sheep farming meant that all over the Highlands, landlords were clearing the glens of people, some of them quite ruthlessly with the help of troops, burning the thatched cottages in which their tenants lived. Canada was the most obvious alternative to the growing industrial towns of the mainland, and emigration soon came to be organised, partly by landlords anxious to get rid of their people, and partly by those who had acquired large tracts of virgin land in Canada and wished to have them settled. By the time the Arran leases of 1814 were expiring, the settlement of Canada was in full swing.

Many people displaced from their homes in Arran must have gone to the mainland to find work, often in the appalling conditions prevailing in the early years of the Industrial Revolution, but of them there is no record.

Nor is there any record of emigration to Canada of the people cleared from Margareoch, Glenree, Burican, Gargadale, Corriehiam and Glenscorrodale in the Sliddery glen, or from Cloined, Aucheleffan, Strathgail, Ballygonachie and Auchareoch on the Kilmory water – a distressing catalogue of townships where generations of islanders had raised their families and lived out their lives. It is thought that many of these folk went to Chaleur Bay, opposite Prince Edward Island, but the records are poor.

We do have a record of the Clearances from the north end of the island, however, when all the people from the farms there, at South, Mid, and North Sannox, the Laggantuine, the Laggan, the Cuithe and the Cock

Burial ground, two miles south-west of Catacol

were evicted in 1829 to make way for a single large sheep farm at Mid Sannox and a smaller enclosed farm at the Cock. This record is the *Annals of Megantic*, a book written in 1902 by Dugald Mackenzie MacKillop whose father and mother were among the emigrants. The people had early warning of their impending eviction, and started to make preparations for their journey early in 1829. They are said to have taken with them cooking utensils, an abundance of woollen clothing, a few articles of furniture, spinning wheels, tools, seed and some books, mostly religious and including the Gaelic Bible. The emigration had been organised by the estate, and half the fare to Canada – £8 for an adult, or for three children under fifteen – was paid by the 10th Duke of Hamilton.

The first wave of emigrants embarked at Lamlash on 25 April, on a copper-bottomed sailing vessel of 169 tons named the *Caledonia*, and it was perhaps fortunate that the skipper, Captain Donald Millar, was a native of the island. An Independent congregation had been established at Sannox following an evangelical mission in 1800 by the brothers Haldane, and the minister, the Reverend Alexander Mackay, accompanied the people to Lamlash and preached a farewell sermon on the text 'Casting all your care upon Him, for He careth for you'. Twelve families sailed on the *Caledonia*, a passenger load of eighty-six; for five other families, numbering in all twenty-eight, there was no room on the *Caledonia* and on 5 June four of these embarked at Greenock on the *Albion*, and the fifth and last on the *Newfoundland*.

The *Caledonia* was two months at sea, arriving at Quebec on 25 June. A severe storm off the Irish coast caused much distress, all the passengers being violently seasick. Otherwise the more interesting features of the voyage were that the unofficial leader of the group, Archibald MacKillop, held a religious service on deck every Sunday, and that a Paisley weaver was

Previous page: Catacol across Catacol Bay

Right: Giants' graves, Whiting Bay

found stowed away. What might have happened to him in those days we can only guess, but on this occasion the passengers held a *ceilidh* on board and paid his fare from the proceeds.

The *Caledonia* waited two days at Quebec until Captain Millar was able to make arrangements to have it towed up to Montreal, as the passengers were supposed to be bound for Renfrew County in Upper Canada. After disembarking at Montreal they remained at Point St Charles for two weeks, and during this period are said to have dealt with a huge amount of washing along the shores of the St Lawrence. It was during this period, too, that they were approached by the Quebec immigration agent, who recommended that they should go to Megantic County in Lower Canada, instead of to the destination originally planned.

His motive for this suggestion is said to have been that he wanted to have Megantic peopled by fellow Scots as a means of securing votes when he stood for election as the county representative; he did in fact contest the seat in 1832, though unsuccessfully. Archibald MacKillop adopted his suggestion, however, and along with William Kelso went to view the proposed ground, on which they were able to report favourably. So the passengers took a barge back down the river to Point St Nicholas, about fifteen miles (24km) from Quebec on the south side of the river, at a cost of two dollars a head. French-Canadian teamsters then transported them, at the rate of five dollars per horse-load of passengers and luggage, over some forty to fifty miles (64–80km), a journey which took two days, to a ford on a river named the Thames, which lay close to the area in which the new land was to be allocated.

They arrived at the ford in the middle of July and set up their tents, but it was to be six weeks before a government agent arrived to allocate the land, which had been surveyed in 1819 and the 100 acre (40 hectare) lots numbered. It is said that the heads of families, and the sons over twenty-one years of age, had been promised a lot each. There was some disappointment, then, when the sons got nothing, even though Archibald MacKillop got 200 acres (80 hectares), and the heads of families 100 acres (40 hectares) each. They settled on their new land, which was virgin forest, on the first of September, rather late in the year to clear much of the land for the next spring sowing, and the six weeks lost at the ford were no doubt regretted.

The stay at the ford was saddened also by an epidemic which caused the death of two of the children, Jane MacKillop, an infant of two, and Margaret Kelso, aged fifteen. But it was gladdened a little by the arrival of the families which had crossed the Atlantic from Greenock, so that by the time the tents were struck at the ford the company consisted of seventeen families from the north end of Arran, numbering in all 117 people. Later the Arran settlers in Megantic were to be joined by others from the island, for between 1830 and 1843 seventeen more families arrived, mostly in small groups, so that by the end of the period the Scotch Settlement, as it was called, had a population of 222.

The severe Canadian winter was a shock to the settlers and there were two deaths: Neil Walker who was over eighty when he sailed with his daughter in the *Caledonia*, and the elderly widow MacKillop, who had sailed on the *Albion* with her six children. Meanwhile the work on clearing the forest was held up by the intense frost, although some of the younger men took advantage of the break to earn wages in the timber mills at Ottawa. By February the average clearing was four acres (1.6 hectares), Archibald MacKillop having twenty (8 hectares) to his credit. With the harvest from these, the emigrants had their first income – apart from the wages earned in Ottawa – since their last Arran harvest of 1828, a gap of two years.

One wonders, in view of the contempt poured on the communal farms by some of the 'improvers', how they managed to acquire the savings to pay their travelling expenses, maintain themselves between the two harvests, and stock their new holdings, The answer no doubt lies partly in the money obtained from the sale of their Arran stock, but it is also clear that they cannot have been destitute. Nor were they enfeebled in constitution by intermarriage, as is sometimes suggested by people who, noticing the preponderance of MacKillops, Kelsos, MacKinnons, Mackenzies and Kerrs among the emigrants, fail to realise that among the Highland people a common surname does not necessarily imply a very close relationship. The hardships they endured from the long sea voyage and the drastic change in climate were great, but out of the 117 people involved in the first wave of settlement only four failed to survive the journey and the first testing winter, one of them a man over eighty and another a mere infant. Their very survival is proof that they were hardy.

The people took with them their passion for religion. Archibald MacKillop held services at his house until a log meeting-house was built in 1832, but after that there was a minister, Donald Henry, who had left Arran the year before. By 1840 the settlers had built a Congregational chapel. Although in wood, it had a striking resemblance to the Independent chapel built by the emigrants in 1822 before they left Sannox, which is now the Congregational church there. The Haldane evangelists of 1800 had affected the Sannox people deeply, and the emigrants had carried with them their tendency to be overscrupulous in sectarian matters. It is recorded that they were at first troubled in Canada as to whether they ought to allow the bowls for collecting maple syrup to remain in position on the sabbath, although to remove them would lead to waste. The problem was solved for them when they remembered that the Lord allowed the corn to grow on the sabbath, and they did not then hesitate to accept the benefit. The problem of when to break the pond ice for Sunday's water, which was frozen in the bucket if carried in on Saturday, also gave rise to two schools of thought.

These experiences must have been, in general, similar to those of Highland settlers everywhere, but we are fortunate in having these records of what happened to the folk from Arran, and there are not many other settlements which give us such detail of everyday life in the New World.

Overleaf: Beach at Kildonan looking to Bennan Head

CLIMATE AND VEGETATION

WARM AND WET WEATHER

The climate is mild because of the warming influence of the Gulf Stream; and wet because of the moisture-laden character of the prevailing south-westerly wind which blows in from the Atlantic, and being impeded very little by the low land of Kintyre, meets the Arran peaks with its load unshed. The rainfall in the higher central area of the island must average 80–100 inches (200–250cm) in a year. At Dougrie, on the west coast, the average is 46 inches (116cm), and at Brodick, on the east, it is 65–70 inches (165–177cm), so the east is rather wetter than the west, which is to be expected, since the wind unloads its moisture only when the hills are reached.

AFTER THE CLOSE of the glacial period the climate of Arran changed at first to cold and wet, and then, when the sea level had fallen to below that of today, to continental, with warm dry summers and cold winters. During that period of the 25 foot (7.6m) beach the climate was insular, that is, mild and wet, and milder and wetter than that of today. As the sea level fell again two further changes followed, to cold and dry, and finally to mild and wet which is the climate of today. These changes would be of mere academic interest if they had left no mark on the island's vegetation, but they initiated many of the tree species which have survived into the present. They were also responsible for the formation of the peat which covers so much of the high inland area, because much of the tree growth which flourished during the dry continental period was destroyed by moss during the subsequent very wet period of the 25 foot (7.6m) beach. This great blanket of peat covers the surface of the 1,000 foot (300m) plateau around the northern peaks and also its declining extension to the south, and determines the vegetation of most of the island. Elsewhere the determining factors are the mass of boulder clay deposited during the glacial period at the tail of the Arran ice stream in the south-west of the island, the mixed soils worn from the rocks by the waters and burns and deposited in the straths, the sandy gravels of the 25 foot (7.6m) beach, and of course the climate itself.

Though the south-westerly wind means rain, this is usually in the form of showers, with bright intervals between. The wind which brings most continuous rain, accompanied by overcast skies, is from the south, blowing warmly in July and early August, and mildly and frequently in winter. The east wind in summer brings dry grey weather to the east of the island, but leaves the west under blue skies; in winter it can carry in snow, although usually to the higher ground. In March it is a cold drying wind, when it blows so regularly that it can be relied upon to prepare the ground for early sowing. The north wind prevails in May and June, and brings cool sunny weather; in winter when it is common, it establishes a pattern of cold sunny days and frosty nights. A north-west wind is normal for November and April, and seldom blows below gale force, bringing battering showers of cold rain.

Average daily temperatures show that July is the warmest month, with a maximum of 64°F (17.5°C), but June has high maximum and minimum temperatures as well, with the lowest rainfall and the most sunshine. January and February are the coldest months, with an average minimum of just under 36°F (2.2°C). The maximum rainfall occurs between November and January, and the minimum between May and June. Frost can be expected between the middle of November and the middle of March, but is seldom severe.

Wind force and exposure to the sun vary considerably in an island of such rugged relief, with so many steep precipices, corries, scarps and deep

Right: Merkland Point with Holy Island visible in the distance

PLANTATIONS

Most of the other trees growing around the low-lying cultivated and inhabited areas are the result of planting, and include sycamore, beech, chestnut, elm, lime and Scots pine. Several nineteenth-century plantations of spruce or larch grow up some of the hillsides in stark unnatural squares and oblongs, as in Glenrosa and Glenshurig, at Corrygills, Glenashdale and Whitefarland, and between the lower reaches of the Sannox and North Sannox burns. Some of these are now being felled. In pleasing contrast are the more recent plantings of the Forestry Commission, in Glencloy and on the higher ground in the middle and south of the island, where a variety of trees have been planted to suit the soil, resulting in a pattern which, while differing in its colours from that of the open hillside, has nevertheless a much more acceptable affinity with the natural surroundings.

glens. The northern peaks, high southern moorlands and the west coast are sometimes violently windswept, as are the glens which open to the west and north and consequently funnel the gales. Snow lies throughout the winter in the corries facing north, and often on the highest peaks, even in bright sunshine. The lonely north coast, the deep fjord-like depression containing Lochranza, the southern slopes of the glens which run from east to west, or west to east, have little or no sunshine for several months in the winter. On the other hand, hillsides with a southern exposure, the northern slopes of the glens just mentioned, and the coast around the southern part of the island, enjoy a full winter as well as summer of sunshine, and where the southern exposure is accompanied by shelter from the prevailing wind, as at Lagg near the mouth of the Kilmory water, conditions can be almost sub-tropical.

These local variations, in conjunction with the variety of soils, sustain a range of vegetation including at one extreme the unique Arran whitebeam or service trees, and palm trees at the other. The service trees are to be found at a height of about 900 feet (275m) in Glen Diomhan, a glacial hanging valley which runs north-westward to meet Glen Catacol about two miles (3.2km) from the sea; and in the upper reaches of North Sannox burn, about half a mile (800m) below Coire na Ceum, under the great chasm of Ceum na Caillich. The trees are of two varieties, *Sorbus arranensis* and *Sorbus pseudo-fennica*. They are related to the rowan, but seem to survive in situations which the rowan could not tolerate, hanging precariously by the tips of their roots to cracks in the granite almost wholly devoid of soil.

Of the other indigenous trees the rowan, although requiring more soil than the service trees, grows at higher levels. Isolated rowan trees in the glens of Arran often indicate an abandoned cottage nearby for one of the properties of the rowan is to dispel evil spirits. Birch grows plentifully on the steep sides of the glens, mixed with hazel lower down. Scrubby oak grows thinly on the lower hillsides, and ash, hawthorn and holly are common at the margins of abandoned fields or in formerly inhabited hollows. Alder and willow appear by the banks of streams and burns as they come closer to sea level, and there are odd clumps of blackthorn.

Where the land is open to the predations of grazing animals, the trees survive only in the steep sides of the glens, or very thinly in areas where stocking has not been intense, as on the hillsides north of Corrie, south of Lochranza, and east of Pirnmill. The grazing animals on the higher ground are red deer and blackface sheep, the latter an eighteenth-century import. Although the deer are indigenous they are to some extent husbanded for purposes of sport, the island north of the Glenshurig and Machrie waters being fenced off as deer forest and the animals protected from all but stalkers. The deer forest has also been managed to encourage the red grouse – though less so recently – which feed mainly on heather, normally controlled by burning. So the vegetative pattern of the unplanted hillside, commonly considered 'natural', is perhaps no more so than that of the new forests since it, too, is considerably affected by human intervention: that of the shepherd

The Cat Stone

and gamekeeper. It is, however, more familiar to the older generation, and therefore more congenial to them: it certainly gives great aesthetic pleasure.

The summits and ridges of the north are mainly of bare rock and coarse granite sand, but the tops of the shoulders encircling the corries nourish a mat of sedges, mosses and lichens, with rare plants of purple and starry saxifrage, alpine willow, crowberry and cloudberry. Heather grows among the tumbles boulders in the corries, accompanied by some blaeberry, and continues down the steep slopes below to the level of about 1,500 feet (457m), where, if the ground is less stony, bracken takes its place.

The traditional Arran cottage garden has an apple and a plum tree, some currant and gooseberry bushes, a plot of potatoes, several rows of curly kale, swedes and leeks, a row of lettuces and spring onions, and some parsley. These suit the soil and weather and require little effort. Some of the larger gardens extend their range to include a row of raspberry canes and a bed of strawberries. Flowers are usually confined to the vicinity of the gate, footpath and front door: the most memorable are snowdrops, crocuses and daffodils, which because of the mild winters flower unusually early. Today the traditional cottage garden is on the decline, and the trim suburban garden, confined mainly to lawn and flowers, is on the increase, and indeed predominates in the main villages.

8 ARRAN'S BACK DOOR
Lochranza and the Lords of the Isles

Lochranza Castle

CONTINUING NORTH from Catacol, it is only one more mile (1.6km) to Lochranza. From this road there are excellent views across Kilbrannan Sound to Kintyre; on a clear day you should be able to pick out the imposing castle of Skipness. Before reaching the village you pass the 'Sailor's Grave' where a plaque can be found to John MacLean who died in 1854.

The old ferry pier is long closed, but the new slipway for the seasonal ferry from Claonaig has rescued Lochranza from its fate as a sleepy backwater. This service has proved extremely popular, and the ferries now in use are much larger than the original tiny 'landing craft' which could only hold six cars.

The setting of the village of Lochranza is extremely picturesque, and greatly improved by Lochranza Castle on a promontory. There is a youth hostel in the village.

Pages 90–1: Lochranza Castle at sunset

LOCHRANZA CASTLE

AS AT SKIPNESS across the water, the first castle at Lochranza was a hall house. It is likely to have been built in the middle of the thirteenth century, like Skipness, in the territory of the Lords of the Isles, the descendants of Somerled. Documentary records are skimpy, but probably the MacSweens of Knapdale had it constructed and we know that it was in possession of Dugald MacSween in 1261. The chief residence of the MacSweens was at Castle Sween, on Loch Sween in Knapdale; they have certainly left their mark in local place-names!

However, by the time of King Hakon's abortive expedition in 1263 which ended with the 'battle' of Largs, the MacSweens were no longer in control of Lochranza, for in 1262 Walter Stewart, Earl of Menteith, had been granted both Arran and Knapdale by his king, Alexander III of Scotland. Since the Stewarts also held Rothesay Castle, their chief stronghold in the area, and also Brodick Castle, it is not clear to what use they put their newly acquired fortress at Lochranza.

On the death of John Stewart who had no heir, the Arran castles passed to Robert the High Steward who became King of Scotland in 1371: from that date Arran's castles became royal castles although they were never royal residences. In 1452 the tenant was Ranald MacAlister, but because he failed to pay his rent, the castle was repossessed by the Crown and given to one of James II's favourites, Alexander, Lord Montgomery. It remained with the Montgomeries, created Earls of Eglinton in 1507, for the next two hundred and fifty years, passing to the Hamiltons in 1705 as the result of the foreclosure of a mortgage. At some time in the late sixteenth century one of the Montgomeries had the hall house converted into a tower house, the ruins of which we see today. It is interesting that whereas the Montgomeries had their L-shaped house facing the land, the earlier MacSween hall house was built facing the sea, from where their power and influence came.

A full architectural description of Lochranza Castle can be found in an excellent Historic Scotland booklet, *The Ancient Monuments of Arran*.

RELIGIOUS WARS

THE KINGDOMS of Scotland and England were united in 1603 when James VI succeeded Elizabeth, taking the title of James I. As regards religion, episcopacy was established in 1606. In 1615 there was a charter of the church lands of Shiskine to James, 2nd Marquis of Hamilton, by his kinsman Andrew, the Protestant bishop of Argyll. Church lands in Sannox, thought to have been granted at one time to the monastery of Kilwinning, may at this time have fallen into the hands of the Montgomeries: thus the Reformation had enabled the nobility in Arran – as in other parts of Scotland – to deprive the new church of lands which had been the main source of the old church's revenue.

SANNOX AND CORRIE

At the head of Lochranza – 'Kendloch of Ransay' in the 1452 charter to the Montgomeries – the road runs up a now deserted glen, over the watershed and down the 'Boguille' towards North Sannox. On the left are deserted settlements, victims of the Clearances. There is a Farm Park at North Sannox, which is advertised as having the only llama on the island – the ones on Holy Isle have only one 'l'. In the village of Sannox itself there is a long stretch of sandy beach; this is the starting point for walks up Sannox Glen.

The next village down the coast, Corrie, is one of the most picturesque settlements on the island, with a general store, post office and craft shop. High Corrie is one of the best examples of a surviving clachan, *the traditional cluster of whitewashed houses which made up the settlement of the old communal farming system.*

Grave of Edwin Rose at Sannox. He was murdered on Goatfell

This was an unsettled period in Arran's history, and it is difficult to discern any evidence of consistent adherence by its people to any particular sectarian principle. The truth is, they were obliged to resist their landlords' enemies whatever the beliefs they may have nourished in the privacy of their own minds. The Hamiltons, although vacillating, were predominantly Royalist, while their neighbours across the water to the north, the Campbells, were Covenanters. In 1639, when the 2nd Marquis of Hamilton was representing Charles I in his dealings with the Covenanters, a party of Campbells, on the order of Argyll, invaded the island and seized Brodick Castle. If they left a garrison behind it may have been withdrawn during the devastating campaign of the Royalist Marquis of Montrose, who had the MacDonalds of Dunivaig in his army. One of these, Alister MacDonald, also known as Young Colkitto, was a special terror to his enemies, and when on the defeat of Montrose at Philliphaugh the survivors of his army returned to their own territories, there was consternation among the Montgomery dependants in Lochranza Castle.

Widened bridge at Sannox

In 1646 a Campbell garrison was again in Brodick Castle; they were under siege by islanders loyal to the Hamiltons, when a party of Campbells was sent to relieve it, in a raid of extraordinary savagery. In a complaint made after the Restoration it is said that the Campbells:

> entered imediatly upon the saids inhabitants theair cattel,
> nolt sheip & bestiall and put them aboard thair saids vessells
> and transported tham as many of them therein as they could
> carry over and killed and destroyed the rest they could not
> transport; and did flay those whilk they killed and tooke
> away thair hyds and skins amounting in all the killed
> destroyed & transported bestiall to the number of two
> thousand kyne or therabout besides their pillageing of
> what other pettie goods moveable the bounds did afford,
> and rivined the houses & cottages.

Previous page: Glen Sannox with Cioch na h-Oighe on the left

According to the same account, the lands of Arran lay waste after this foray for a space of six years. The suffering must have been appalling.

INDUSTRIES

FOR SOUND GEOLOGICAL REASONS, the north end of the island has always had more quarrying and industrial enterprises. At the end of the eighteenth century John Burrel explored the possibilities of the local stone at the glen farm near Lochranza, and for a time slate was indeed quarried here. By the end of the century limestone was being quarried at Corrie.

J.A.Thomas, woodturner, Kilmory

In the earlier half of the nineteenth century there were carding mills at Brodick and Burican, a flax mill at Lagg, and a waulking and dye mill at Monamore. We have already mentioned the bobbin mill at Pirnmill, and there was a clay drain tile manufactory at Clauchog. In 1793 there had been three licensed distilleries on the island, but in 1836 the last of them, at Torrylin, had closed, and the Arran barley was sent to Campbeltown. Similarly, more efficient equipment resulted in the closure of three meal mills – in around 1811 there were five, reduced to two in 1878: one at Shedog, the ruin of which is still visible, and the other, a distinguished red sandstone building with crow-stepped gables, situated downstream from the dye mill at Monamore. By 1909 the Shedog miller was superintending both mills until they closed a few years later. The lovely Monamore mill was a striking feature of the landscape even in ruin; however, it became unsafe and was demolished in 1967.

The mining of coal and quarrying of slate in the Lochranza area did not survive into the nineteenth century, but the quarrying of white sandstone and limestone continued at Corrie, above the port and below An Sgriob, and of limestone in the Clauchan glen. Local limestone was burnt in kilns both at Corrie and Shiskine. Imported white Irish limestone was burnt at Clauchog. During World War 1 a very pure limestone was quarried beside the Coire nan Larach burn, north-north-west of High Corrie, and a tramline conveyed it to the Corrie Sandstone Quay. This quay was built originally in 1882 to serve the red sandstone quarry further south, and was connected with it by a light railway. Red sandstone was also quarried at Brodick, Cordon, and Monamore, and there was some quarrying of building stone in the schists at Lochranza and in quartz-porphyry at Glenree and Brown Head. The red sandstone quarries were the longest in use, although by 1928

Blacksmith at the Isle of Arran Heritage Museum, Brodick

GOAT'S MILK AND ROMANCE

The first holidaymakers on record seem to have come just after the middle of the eighteenth century, by the weekly sailing packet from Saltcoats, to drink goat's milk, then fashionable as a health beverage, in a 'commodious slated house hard by the castle of Brodick'; this must refer to the building now known as the Cladach, said to have been built by the Duchess Anne early in the eighteenth century for her physician, and afterwards extended and converted for use as an inn. It is said to have been the first slated house in Brodick, and was for a long time known as Tigh an Sgleat for that reason. There is evidence also that Paisley weavers – the aristocracy of the labouring classes before the power loom reduced them to penury – came to the black-houses in the old clachan *of Glenrosa during the same period also to drink goat's milk, and to ramble in the glen and round about the slopes of Goatfell. In time, goat's milk lost popularity; besides which it became difficult to obtain since the goat was discouraged by the improving factors of the nineteenth century – the fashion which brought the succeeding wave of holidaymakers was that for romantic scenery.*

were being abandoned. Bits of Arran red sandstone can be found in medieval chapels and castles throughout Argyll, most memorably in Skipness Castle.

Barytes was first mined at Sannox in 1840, and between 1853 and 1862 nearly 5,000 tons were produced, but the mine was closed by the 11th Duke of Hamilton on the grounds that it spoiled the solemn grandeur of the scene. After World War I it was reopened, and a wooden pier and light railway built. By 1934 the output had risen to 9,000 tons, but the vein petered out in 1938. The pier and light railway were demolished at the close of World War II.

Mining and quarrying maintained the bulk of the population of Corrie and Sannox from the time of the Clearances until just before the beginning of World War I; there was also fishing, which employed a fair number of people in the main villages throughout the nineteenth century; but apart from these, the industries of the island did little to provide work for the people displaced from farms by 'improved' methods. The island might have been seriously denuded of people had not advances in methods of transport made travel more comfortable, speedier and cheaper, therefore bringing country and seaside holidays gradually within reach of those obliged to spend the greater part of the year in the unpleasant environment of the new industrial towns. Even so, it was some time before manual workers and labourers could afford holidays, and although with the extension of the franchise and the growth of trade unions wages began to rise in the mills and factories, Arran was still beyond the means of all but the middle classes and the aristocracy; it was therefore as a resort for the latter that it developed in the second half of the nineteenth century.

Today's visitors have their own motives, and perhaps some day a visiting anthropologist will record the interaction between native islanders, incomers, and tourists which provides so much interest and entertainment for all concerned – as well as a good living for those in tourist-related enterprises. Readers who have followed us around the coasts of Arran in these chapters may find it helpful to visit the Arran Heritage Museum for further information, if they are fortunate enough to be on the island. Armchair travellers will have to make do with the assistance of their local library – many books have been written about Arran, a few of which are listed at the end of this one. Whichever kind of traveller you are, we hope that you will return to Arran again and again, to explore its past, enjoy its present, and contribute to its future.

9 WALKS AND EXCURSIONS

ACCESS

BEFORE DESCRIBING some possibilities for walking excursions on Arran, a brief word about rights of access. Basically, access (on foot) to the countryside in Arran, and to all historic sites, is unrestricted, bounded only by considerations of courtesy and common sense. It is sensible to ask directions, if not permission. Any advice offered should be followed, and visitors should take particular care not to damage dykes and fences, and to avoid disturbing stock, especially in the lambing season. Even the sight of an unfamiliar dog can upset sheep, so visitors should keep their pets well away from sheep, or at the very least under close control, preferably on a leash.

Freedom of access does not give visitors the right to tamper with historic sites without the owner's permission. Similarly, visitors must apply to the appropriate authorities for permits to fish. Hotels and the Tourist Information Centre in Brodick can offer advice about where to apply. The same applies to anybody wishing to fish for salmon or to shoot game. Doing these things without permission is poaching, and is illegal. It is also dangerous.

So, although there are no laws prohibiting rights of access, there has to be some give and take with landowners and farmers. Their livelihood is often at stake, as well as other people's jobs.

EQUIPMENT

VISITORS ALWAYS HOPE for good weather, but in our climate there are no guarantees, only wishful thinking, and in the absence of a direct line to the Almighty certain precautions are essential. The key elements in Arran's weather are wetness, and wind. Even when the sky is blue and the hill-lochs are shimmering with scenic beauty, the ground underfoot is likely to be boggy once off roads and tracks. Adequate raingear and correct footwear will make it possible to have a good time, whatever the weather. Inadequate protection leads inevitably to saturation, cold, misery, recriminations and regret, especially where small children are concerned. Wet clothing can be dried out – eventually – but without doubt prevention is the best cure. Even

MIDGES

Basically, nothing can be done about midges. Some people think they are sent by Divine Providence as punishment, and when you are suffering because of them this sometimes seems the only possible explanation. Local shops sell various potions and preparations which, it is claimed, repel midges. Some of these give a measure of short-term protection. The best protection against midges is wind, which fortunately is not in short supply on Arran. So when seeking out a perfect picnic spot or campsite, stay away from damp, sheltered locations!

Pages 98–9: Merkland Point

Pages 100–1: Peaty stream at the top of Glenashdale Falls

on a fine day there is likely to be a brisk breeze, and light, windproof jackets or anoraks should always be carried. The weather can change quickly, often with little warning, and although inadequately clad walkers are unlikely to come to any harm, they can certainly become exceedingly miserable very quickly. Climbers have to take special precautions – don't venture on to difficult routes on the high mountains unless you are experienced, well-equipped, and familiar with mountain landscapes and the respect they demand.

Correct footwear is most important. Proper walking boots with Vibram soles are best, and need not be expensive or heavy. Good walking shoes are acceptable only for farm tracks or beachcombing expeditions. Trainers will become soaked in anything but drought conditions and can be ruined quickly and easily. Wellies are uncomfortable to walk in for any distance, and are positively dangerous in wet conditions. If you buy new boots or shoes for your island adventure, try to break them in first, or come well provided with plasters to deal with the inevitable blisters.

CORRIE – GOATFELL – BRODICK CASTLE (6 HOURS)

THIS IS THE 'CLASSIC' Arran walk, about 8 miles (12.8km) in length and well within the capabilities of anybody in reasonable physical condition, of any age.

The walk starts from the village of Corrie, 4 miles (6.4km) north of Brodick, where there is a car park opposite the road leading to High Corrie. Do not attempt to drive up the farm road. Walk up the farm track, and go through a gate on the left just before the first house at High Corrie. The route is well signposted. At the point where a waterfall on the Corrie Burn is first seen, our path branches off to the right, climbing up the hillside with the burn on the left and a deer fence on the right. The path goes through a gate in the deer fence, then climbs quite steeply for nearly half a mile (800m), after which it levels out into a steady incline up the left bank of the burn.

The village of Corrie

Right: Dun Kilpatrick

The climb up to the ridge at the head of the glen is steep again, so when you arrive there, stop to rest and enjoy the views down Glen Sannox, before turning left (south) and heading for the summit of Goatfell. There are two routes to the top: the lower path is straightforward until the final scramble for the summit, while the higher path, the Stacach route, involves some scrambling and clambering, and is more exciting, without being in the least dangerous.

The view from the top makes the effort worthwhile, so it is best to climb Goatfell on a clear day, if possible. To the north is the dramatic mountain scenery of Arran itself, while off to the west is the Kintyre peninsula, with Islay, Jura and Mull beyond. To the east are the Cumbraes, Bute, the Clyde coast, with Glasgow in the far distance, nestling in front of the Campsies. With keen eyesight, or binoculars, you can just make out the distinctive towers of Glasgow University. To the south is Holy Isle, the rest of Arran, Ailsa Craig and farther off, the coastline of Ireland.

After admiring the view, leave the summit to the south, keeping to the path and taking care amongst the boulder scree. After reaching the Mull Burn, crossed by a small bridge, you are soon back in woodland. The track ends at Brodick Castle. From the main road you can take a bus back to Corrie; timings vary throughout the year, so enquire locally.

LOCHRANZA – LAGGAN – AN SCRIODAN, CIRCULAR WALK (6 HOURS)

THIS IS A CIRCULAR WALK of about 8 miles (12.8km) through dramatic scenery with a sad history: this part of Arran was cleared of its human population to make way for deer and sheep.

From the village of Lochranza, cross the bridge over the Chalmadale Burn, turn left, and park by the shore beyond Lodge Farm. Walk back along the road past Lodge Farm and follow the signpost indicating the track to Laggan. It starts as an easy cart track, but where it drops downhill follow a signposted grassy path which keeps climbing up the slopes of the north side of Glen Chalmadale (see overleaf). The well-worn track crosses a small burn on a wooden bridge and continues to climb steadily. Watch for the 'Sleeping Warrior' (Caisteal Abhail), one of Arran's famous views.

The path crosses a moorland plateau dotted with bog cotton, reaches a ridge, then descends to the shore beside Laggan Cottage. Look for abandoned crofts – on one of these, at Cock Farm, lived the ancestors of Harold Macmillan, who became Prime Minister and the head of a vast publishing empire.

From Laggan Cottage the track winds its way north along the shore. In the eighteenth century coal was mined at Laggan, and the remains of the old harbour can still be seen. Across the sea is the island of Bute, and as the path nears the north point of Arran, the hills of Argyll come into view. Here, t An Scriodan, is a massive sandstone rockfall which occurred 250 years ago, with a roar that could undoubtedly be heard many miles away. Wend your way carefully through the boulders; a little scrambling will be required at times, then the route hugs the shore past Newton Point, finally joining the road at South Newton which leads back into Lochranza.

This walk will be of particular interest to anybody interested in wildlife and natural history, with a varied range of habitats and excellent geology to admire. You should see red deer in the mountains and seals on the shore, ravens and buzzards on the moors, peregrines circling the crags, oyster-catchers and gulls on the coasts, and several species of woodland birds. Rock-hounds can look out for carboniferous coal seams which outcrop near Laggan, also for limestone and sandstone slabs, and the ubiquitous schists.

DRUMADOON AND THE KING'S CAVE FROM BLACKWATERFOOT (3 HOURS)

THIS IS A MOST INTERESTING walk of about 5 miles (8km), with some of the best history, geology, legend and birdlife to be seen anywhere in Scotland.

Follow the signposts for the golf course at Blackwaterfoot, which lies to the west of the village, and park in the public car park there. Go straight to the shore and turn right (west), walking along the sand for half a mile (800m), then turn north up a grassy path, crossing the fence on a stile. To your left is Drumadoon Point, while on your right loom the columnar cliffs of Drumadoon.

From the base of the cliffs continue north, well above the sea shore. You will see the King's Cave in the distance. Continue along the raised beach until you reach the distinctive red sandstone in which the caves were formed when the sea level was higher than it is now. The King's Cave, named after Robert the Bruce – probably erroneously – is marked by iron gates. Go through these into the cavern, and look for the Early Christian carvings on the rock face ahead, on either side of which are dead-end tunnels. It helps to take a torch with you, which can be used both to explore the tunnels and to highlight the carvings. Fulmars nest on the cliffs above.

Retrace your steps towards Drumadoon along the raised beach, watching for the path climbing up the left (north) side of the cliffs to the clifftop. There, go through a gate and cross the ramparts of the massive Iron Age hill fort, once the tribal stronghold of the prehistoric inhabitants of Arran. After exploring the hilltop, return to the gate and continue south. The track goes through bracken to a field with a gate in its right-hand corner. Go through the gate, turn left, and walk along the northern edge of the golf course until you reach a farm track. Here, turn right and follow it back to the car park.

FURTHER POSSIBILITIES

This is just a tiny sample of the possibilities for walks and excursions on Arran. There are forest trails, sheltered walks in the gardens around Brodick Castle, walks along long sandy beaches, and for serious climbers high, difficult summits. The Tourist Information Centre in Brodick usually has leaflets and booklets from which further walks can be planned, or you may want to explore some of the places mentioned earlier in this book. Rock-climbers and mountaineers are well provided for, with specialist guide books and maps.

Please be respectful of the countryside and the people who work in it, equip yourself well, and turn back if the weather deteriorates. It is best to buy the appropriate Ordnance Survey maps, which are on sale in the Tourist Information Centre and elsewhere. The Landranger 1:50,000 map, Sheet 69, is all right for generalised planning, but for serious walking, or for navigating easily to historic or archaeological sites, the Pathfinder series of 1:25,000 maps is essential.

Overleaf: Glen Chalmadale, near Lochranza

Official Loch Ness Monster Exhibition
Drumnadrochit, Inverness-shire IV63 6TU
Tel: 01456 450573
Open daily all year, hours may vary. There is an
admission charge.

Original Loch Ness Monster Exhibition
Drumnadrochit, Inverness-shire IV63 6TU
Tel: 01456 450342/450225
Open daily all year, hours may vary. There is an
admission charge.

National Trust for Scotland Countryside Centre
Torridon, Achnasheen, Ross-shire IV22 2EZ
Tel: 01445 791221
Open 1 May to 30 September, Monday to Saturday
10am to 5pm; Sunday 2pm to 5pm. There is an
admission charge.

Strathnaver Museum
Bettyhill, by Thurso, Sutherland KW14 7SS
Tel: 01641 521421
Open April to October, 10am to 1pm and 2pm to
5pm. There is an admission charge.

Tain Through Time
Tower Street, Tain, Ross-shire IV19 2DY
Tel: 01862 894089
Open April to October, 10am to 5pm. May open by
arrangement outside these times.

Timespan Heritage Centre
Dunrobin Street, Helmsdale, Sutherland KW8 6JX
Tel: 01431 821327
Open April to October, Monday to Saturday 9.30am
to 5pm; Sunday 2pm to 5pm (6pm during July and
August). There is an admission charge.

Ullapool Museum and Visitor Centre
7 & 8 West Argyll Street, Ullapool, Ross-shire
IV26 2TY
Tel: 01854 612987
Open 1 April (or Easter if earlier) to 31 October,
Monday to Saturday 10am to 5pm; 1 October
to 31 March, by prior arrangement with the
Museum Curator.

Urquhart Castle
Nr Drumnadrochit, Inverness-shire IV63 2XJ
Tel: 01456 450551
Open daily October to March 9.30am to 5pm (last
admission); April to September 9.30am to 6pm (last
admission). There is an admission charge.

West Highland Museum
Cameron Square, Fort William, Inverness-shire
PH33 6AJ
Tel: 01397 702169
Open June to September, Monday to Saturday 10am
to 5pm; October to May, Monday to Saturday 10am
to 4pm; Sundays 2pm to 5pm (July & August only)

USEFUL INFORMATION AND PLACES TO VISIT

TOURIST INFORMATION

ourist Information Centre: Brodick, Isle of Arran, KA27 8AU
l: 01770 302140

FERRY SERVICES

ledonian MacBrayne Ltd, The Ferry Terminal, Gourock,
nfrewshire
: 01457 650100 (or 08705 650000 for private vehicles)

PLACES TO VISIT

ran Heritage Museum, Rosaburn, Broderick, KA27 8DP
l: 01770 302636 www.arranmuseum.co.uk

terson Arran Ltd, The Old Mill, Lamlash, KA27 8LE
l: 01770 600606 www.paterson-arran.com

odick Castle, Tel: 01770 302202

orth Sannox Pony Trekking Centre, Sannox
l: 01770 810222

uth Bank Farm, East Brennan, Kildonan
l: 01770 820221

formation on craft shops, outdoor activities, hire of bicycles,
ats and cars, accommodation and restaurants is available from the
ourist Information Centre.

Stained glass maker, Kilmory

FURTHER READING

lfour, J. A. (ed), *The Book of Arran* (Glasgow, 1910)
rrie, R., *The Place-Names of Arran* (Glasgow, 1908)
irhurst, Horace, *Exploring Arran's Past* (Brodick, 1982)
emmell, Alastair, *Discovering Arran* (John Donald, 1990)
e of Arran Tourist Board Arran Visitor Guide
ndsborough, D., *Arran: its Topography, Natural History and Antiquities* (Ardrossan, 1875)
ackenzie, W.M. (ed), *The Book of Arran, vol. 2* (Glasgow, 1914)
ottish Women's Rural Institute, *Arran History of the Villages of the Isle of Arran* (1983)

Left: Paddle steamer Waverley, *the
last sea-going paddle steamer in the
world (Isle of Arran Tourist Board)*

selection of booklets, leaflets and maps is available from the Tourist Information Centre, Brodick.

PLACE-NAMES AND THEIR INTERPRETATION

Beinn Tarsuinn	G. *beinn tarsuinn*	oblique, diagonal mountain
Brodick	N. *breidr vik*	broad bay
Catacol	N. *katta + gil*	ravine of the wild cats
Cioch na h-Oighe	G. *cioch + oigh*	breast of the virgin
Cir Mhor	G. *cir + mor*	the great crest
Cladach	G. *cladach*	at the shore
Clauchlands	G. *clach + lann*	rocky enclosure
Clock of Arran	G. *an coileach*	the cockerel
Corrie	G. *coire*	cauldron
Corriegills	N. *karri + gil*	cock-ptarmigan valley
Dippen	G. *da pheighinn*	twopenny land
Dougrie	G. *dubh garaidh*	dark thicket
Drumadoon	G. *druim + dun*	ridge of the fort
Glen Rosa	G. *gleann* + N. *hross-a*	horse-river valley
Glen Shant	G. *gleann + sianta*	glen of the charm
Goatfell	N. *geit + fiall*	goat mountain
Iorsa	N. *eyrr-a*	gravel-bank river
Kilmory	G. *cill Moire*	the church of Mary
Kiscadale	N. *kistu + dair*	glen of the coffin
Lagg	G. *lag*	a hollow
Lamlash	G. *eilean Molais*	island of Molas
Lochranza	N. *reynis a*	loch of the rowan tree river
Machrie	G. *machair*	coastal field, plain
Monamore	G. *monadh mor*	the big hill
Penrioch	G. *peighinn riabhach*	speckled pennyland
Pirnmill	Sc. *pirn*	mill of the reel, bobbin
Sannox	N. *sand vik*	sandy bay
Shedog	G. *seidheach*	windy place
Shiskine	G. *seasgan*	a marsh
Sliddery	N. *slidor*	slippery
Thundergay	G. *ton re gaoithe*	backside to the wind
Whitefarland	N. *hvitt for-landi*	white land between sea and hill
Whiting Bay		bay of the whiting fish

G. – Gaelic
N. – Norse
Sc. – Scots

INDEX

Page numbers in *italics* indicate ilustrations

Access, 97
Alexander II, 40
Alexander III, 40, 89
Alpine plants, 87
An Scriodan, 104
Architecture, 7
Area, 7
Arran Heritage Museum, 11, 14, *28*, 29, *95*, 96, 109
Arran mustard, 42
Arran Provisions Ltd, 42, *43*, 109

Barbour, John, 19–21, 25
Blackwaterfoot, *66*, 67
Brodick, 7, 10, 29
Brodick Castle, 19–20, 25, 28–9, 94, 104, 109
Bronze Age, 11, 71–2
Brown Head, *9*
Bruce, Robert *see* Robert the Bruce
Bruce, The, 19–21, 25
Bryce, James, 67, 72
Bryce, Thomas, 67
Buddhists, 42
Burns, Robert, 9
Burrel, John, 63
Bus services, 50, 104

Caledonia, 78, 80–1
Caledonian MacBrayne, 10, 47, 109
Campbell atrocities, 94
Canada, 74, 78, 80–1
Castles, 19, 52, 89, *90–1*
Catacol, 74, *74*, *76–7*
Cat Stone, *87*
Chambered cairns, *41*, 45, *79*
Clachans, 58–9, 62, 91
Clearances, 63, 73–4, 96, 104
Climate, 84
Coal mining, 95, 104
Cock Farm, 104
Coire an Lochan, 73
Corrie, 89, 102, *102*
Covenanters, 94
Crops, 59

Dalriada, 32–3
David I, 19
Deer forests, 86–7, 104
Diet, 62
Distilleries, 95
Douglas, Sir James, 20–1
Dougrie Lodge, 73
Drumadoon, 67–8, *69*, 105
Dun Kilpatrick, *103*

Emigrations, 63, 74
Equipment, 99, 102

Farming, 58–9, 62–3
Ferry services, 10, *10*, 47, 88
Feudal system, 19
Fishing, 45
Footwear, 99, 102

Gaelic, 9, 32, 35, 68
Geology, 14–15, 67, 95, 104
Giants' graves, *79*
Glenashdale Falls, *64–5*, *100–1*
Glen Catacol, *75*
Glenchalmadale, *106–7*
Glen Sannox, *92–3*
Glen Shurig, *6*, *48–9*
Goatfell, *6*, *12–13*, *18*, 19, *24*, 25, 91, 96, 102, 104
Goat's milk, 96
Golf courses, *30*, *66*, *70*

Hakon, 40–1, 91
Hamiltons, 28–9, 89, 94
High Corrie, 89, 102
Holy Isle, *30*, 31, 36–7, 40–1, 42, *42–3*, *44*, *85*
Hutton, James, 14

Imachar Point, *73*
Industries, 95
Iron Age population, 67–8

Kelp industry, 74
Kilbride cemetery, *32*, *34*

Kildonan, 52–3, *82–3*
Kilmory, *41*, 53, *54*
Kilpatrick, *50*
King's Cave, 11, *22–3*, 25, 67–8, 105
Kintyre, *9*, 10, 68, 88, 102

Laggan, 104
Lamlash, 7, 9, *30*, 31, *32*, *33*
Landsborough, Rev Dr David, 50–1
Landscape, 9, 72
Largs, Battle of, 40–1
Livestock, 62
Lochranza, 88, 104
Lochranza Castle, 88, *88*, 89, *90–1*
Lords of the Isles, 19, 21, 28, 35–6

MacDonalds, 28, 36
Machrie Moor, 11, *11*, 67, 71–2
Mackay, Rev Alexander, 78
MacKillop, Archibald, 78, 80–1
Macmillan, Harold, 104
MacSweens, 89
Magnus Barelegs, 33
Malcolm II, 36
Maps, 105
Megantic, 80–1
Merkland Point, *85*, *98–9*
Midges, 97
Milner, George, 51
Mining, 95, 96
Montgomeries, 89
Murchies, 41
Museums, 14

National Trust for Scotland, 29
Newton Point, 104
Norse, 9
Norse sovereignty, 33
North Sannox Farm Park, 109

Peat, 72
Piers, 45, 47
Pirnmill, 73
Pitchstone, 15
Place-names, 33